LETTERS FROM NAT

by Nat Wright,
Edited by Sue Wright

RoseDog ❧ Books

PITTSBURGH, PENNSYLVANIA 15222

RoseDog Books
701 Smithfield Street
Pittsburgh, PA 15222
Visit our website at *www.rosedogbookstore.com*

ISBN: 978-1-4349-8677-1
eISBN: 978-1-4349-7673-4

INTRODUCTION

My late husband, Nat Wright, wrote many letters to the home front between March 1945 and June 1946. He graduated from Anacostia High School in Washington, D.C. in February 1945, having already set into motion his enlistment in the Marine Corps. He left graduation ceremonies with his luggage and boarded a bus headed for Parris Island, South Carolina for boot camp. Even though he had the proper papers, he was kicked off the bus and told, "Kid, go home to your Mama!"

Nat was among the most miniscule of WWII Marines, topping off at 5'5". Any time he said otherwise, he *fibbed*! He finally arrived at Parris Island March 1, 1945 and, after boot camp and advanced training at Camp Lejeune, North Carolina, served in the Japanese Allied Occupation Forces and returned to the States in July 1946. These are the letters that his mother, Cass Hoyt Wright, was able to save, usually written to her, sometimes to one of Nat's two sisters: Bonnie, whom Nat called "Runt", almost five, and Pat, 16 when Nat left for boot camp. It is obvious that some letters were not retained.

As you read these letters from the past, remember that Nat enlisted to be a *fighting man*, knowing that as a Marine he would probably be involved in a danger-fraught Japanese invasion. The public did not know about the Atom bomb plans. By a stroke of miraculous luck and timing, he was spared the invasion and the fighting. Instead he had an exceptional experience of travel and adventure, particularly in Japan. As our daughter Beth said on reading the letters, "He always found the upside to everything that he encountered."

Nat was exactly 18 years & three months old when the first of these letters was written. He knew vaguely that he wanted a career in journalism or the arts. He at one time aspired to be a political cartoonist and I think he would have been an excellent one. He eventually had a 40-year career as a radio broadcaster, with some TV exposure. These letters are incredibly descriptive and interesting for such a young man to have written. I don't remember, during my days of receiving letters from young G.I.s, including my own genius-rated brother, any enlisted man who turned a phrase or told a story as well as this enthusiastic 18-year-old.

Nat spent summers on a family farm on the Eastern Shore of Maryland from the time he was a small child. He and his cousins were the hard-working farmhands. That is how his extended family made it through the Great Depression with enough to feed everyone. His many comments about his cousins, aunts and uncles in these letters refer mainly to those with whom he spent those pastoral summers. They had all bonded to the extent that they were psychologically more like siblings than cousins.

The letters are written on an assortment of whatever paper he could get hold of, in sloppy pen and ink or pencil, which was neater, but has become, with age, increasingly difficult to decipher. I present them basically as written, with editing of only spelling, obvious errors and omissions. The only way he could correct errors in pen & ink was to scratch them out. This transcript of his letters has been done by me as a posthumous gift of love to Nat, who died at 82 in 2009 shortly after our 55th wedding anniversary and our 58th year together. I was aware of these letters and often encouraged Nat to "do something" with them, but he never did. He did not offer them to me to read. I do not know why. Perhaps he thought them sophomoric; they are anything but. His family and friends have much enjoyed these sometimes humorous, sometimes serious and often poetic letters. I hope you, the reader, will, too.

Just think, our troops now carry laptops into alien territory & send their messages home so easily, instantly & neatly. But what will they have of those messages 65 years from now? I love having these letters to remember the youthful Nat I didn't even know.

(My comments, changes or additions in Italics in this small print. I am glad that 18-year-old Nat & I didn't know each other in 1945, as I was then 11 years old. Our 58-year liaison would not have happened!)

Nat's wife, *Sue Wright* August 2010

Dedicated to
Nat's mother
Cass Wright

(This is the first saved letter. I am sure many letters were passed on to friends or family members & not retrieved)

(Parris Island S.C.)
(Sat.) Mar. 10, 1945

Dear Mother,

I've been a Marine boot for over a week now and so far everything is turning out OK. We're kept pretty much on the go, but that doesn't hurt me any. In fact, it'll probably do me a lot of good, because, by nature, I'm one of the laziest guys in the world. Down here the days are warm and balmy and the nights are cool, turning chilly toward morning. We roll out at 5 A.M. every morning and, believe me, it sure feels a lot like getting up to go milking down on the farm.

The trees are practically all green down here and there are quite a few palm trees, most of which line the streets. We are quartered in long, round-roofed huts, somewhat like the ones we pass on the way to Sandy Point.

We have to swab the decks and bulkheads (that's Marine jargon for floors and walls) every day. They sure showed me how to wield a mean swab and I've developed quite a domestic touch (maybe I should have joined the WAMs). Believe me, our uniforms, and I use the term "uniforms" loosely, consisting of olive drab fatigue dungarees, are nothing like those glamorous ones they show on recruiting posters. We've been fitted for dress greens, but we can only wear them to church and when we leave boot camp. I'll be here for about 8 or 9 weeks and then shove off for Camp Lejeune. I more than likely will get a furlough within a very short while after reaching Camp Lejeune, so I should be home at least during the latter part of May. That's not definite, but it's a pretty good possibility.

The trip down from Washington was pretty rugged. We rode down in a dirty day coach with a crowd of fellows from Boston. We were pretty cramped and didn't get much sleep. I sure was stiff, tired and grimy when we changed over to the Marine Corps train at Yamasee, S.C. I didn't see much of North Carolina, as we traveled through it during the night. However, I did see a lot of the beautiful scenery in the Virginia foothills, as there was a bright full moon. But in North Carolina it was cloudy and turned pitch dark. I saw a good deal of South Carolina the next morning. It sure seemed funny to see green grass and blossoms after leaving chilly and bare D.C. It's like spring down here.

We have quite a few married men in our platoon, in fact just about half. There are several men over thirty, two of them 35 and 36 respectively. Also we have, among others, a football coach, a pro football player, a song writer, a school teacher and a former Annapolis midshipman in our midst. Some platoon, eh?

Say, please send me *(Cousins)* Dinny's and Sud's addresses, will ya?

Well, I've gotta hit the sack now. I'll write again as soon as possible. When you get a chance, please send some stationery, as our PX is out. I think I may have asked for some in my last letter. If so, disregard this request.

So long for now.

Love to all, Bunk

P.S. Have you received my last letter yet? I mailed it in a hurry and may have misaddressed it.

(In the South, Bunk was a common nickname for a first or only son. Nat's parents & sister Bonnie called him Bunk. Sister Pat called him Nat, as did his friends, schoolmates & teachers. Granny, God bless her, called him Nathaniel! His full name was Nathaniel van Wert Wright, IV.)

****

(Parris Island S.C.)
(Thu.) Mar. 15, 1945

Dear Pat,

I'm on my tenth training day today and they keep us hustling most all the time. I've been here about two weeks, but our official training didn't start till four days after we got here. However, we didn't exactly loaf those first four days. Our first day, we got a going over by Lou Diamond when we changed from civvies to G.I. clothes. He's a pretty rough character. Our uniforms consist of green dungarees and G.I. brogans. I look like a fugitive from a rummage sale.

You probably won't notice it, but there's been a slight pause of two days between this sentence and the last. Today is the 17th and I'm on my 12th training day. I left off on Wednesday at the part about the rummage sale. I was interrupted by chow call and have been so busy since, my trips to the head have been dive-bomber fashion, that is, in again and out again on the run without slowing down.

I'm writing this while waiting to go on guard duty. I have a two-hour watch tonight. We had an inspection by a battalion officer today. He asked questions on just about everything we have learned so far: first aid, guard duty, USMC history, rifle nomenclature and other subjects. He asked one West Virginia hillbilly in the 2nd squad a first-aid question. The question was, "What is shock?" The prize-winning answer was, "Bad news from home, sir." Gee, we got some eight balls in our platoon. A couple fellows had rust on their rifles, so we will probably have to work tomorrow. Mine was clean as a whistle but that doesn't make any difference to our D.I. If one guy fools around, the whole platoon gets it in the neck.

I served on guard duty yesterday. I was acting Corporal of the Guard. When I went to report for duty, the Sergeant of the Guard gave me a quizzical look and asked me who forged my papers saying I was old enough to get in.

Don't let anybody kid you. *(Anacostia High School)* Cadet training really pays off in the end. Most of our time here is taken up with close-order drill and I got somewhat of a head start on the other fellows because of the foundation I got in the Cadets. I sure am glad I joined that outfit in school. It's really going tough on a lot of guys who never had any previous training of any kind..

We have a pretty square shooter for a corporal. He can be plenty tough, but he'll give you a break when you deserve one. All the fellows like him. I don't think his opinion of me is any too high, however. The other night I asked him if he ever lost his belt on Haines Point in Washington. *(This was a naughty thing for Nat to write to his younger sister.)* It's a darn good thing he was in a good humor that day or my mail might have been forwarded to the brig.

Say, I was wondering if sometime you might be able to send me an old copy of Reader's Digest. Just any old copy would be swell. It would make swell reading for a long time and I could pass it around the platoon. We're not allowed big, gaudy magazines like Pic, Life, Look, etc. Also, comic books are frowned upon. Our D.I.s just don't appreciate thirst for culture. However, small, pocket-sized books and magazines are all right.

You better brace yourself for this. I have been to church the last two Sundays in a row and I have an appointment with the chaplain to see about getting confirmed. Shocking, isn't it?

Gotta quit for now. The head beckons (ugh!).

Love to all, Nat

P.S. I'm now sporting a ¼ -inch growth of hair (Bald bastard, ain't I?).

****

(Parris Island S.C.)
(Sun.) April 1, 1945

Dear Mother,

I guess you were wondering when this no good boot of a son of yours was gonna up and write. Honest, I would have sooner, but last week we moved from the main station to new quarters out on the rifle range, and they've kept us pretty busy our first week out here. We have completed 3 weeks of preliminary training consisting mostly of close-order drill and plenty of deck swabbing. Believe me, Cadet training really paid off with that close-order drill. I was appointed a squad leader and also serve as platoon guide.

We have now begun 4 weeks of training in how to shoot the M-1 rifle, the Browning Automatic Rifle and the carbine. Also, we will learn how to toss grenades. For the past week we have been practicing snapping into the firing positions and firing the .22 in preparation for the firing of the three named weapons. The rifle instructors are always ribbing me about my size. Whenever I take a position on the firing line, they will always yell, "Hey, rifle, where you takin' that boy?"

The other night some fellows were clowning around in the chow line, so our corporal made us stage a field day. A field day here consists of the scattering of sand and water over the barracks floor, followed by a thorough scrubbing of the floor by the whole platoon. Each man has to carry in a bucket of sand and a bucket of water and dump it on the floor. Well it seems we got bored with carrying water, so we proceeded to have a water battle. It started with just two fellows, and pretty soon the whole platoon joined in, sousing each other by the bucket-load. Then came the crowning touch. Our corporal intervened in an attempt to break it up and was subsequently soused with 3 bucket-loads at once. Luckily, however, he was in a good humor and was able to grin and bear it. The only repercussion was being called a few choice names. Honest, it was the most fun I've had since I came here.

Hey, by the way, I thought you might like to know: I've put on about 6 pounds so far, maybe more. I'm pretty sure I'll gain more as I go along. I may have grown a little, I don't know. At any rate it would be hard to tell because we have quite a few 6-footers (one guy is 6 feet 5) and in comparison to them I look like a midget.

Boy, I'll sure be one happy guy when my 10-day furlough rolls around about the last part of May. I miss you and Pop and Pat and the "Runt" *(5-year-old sister Bonnie)* like the dickens. Also I miss that old

Victrola. Whenever I get a chance to go to the PX, I establish a beachhead on the juke-box. While the other fellows are crowding up to the cigarette counter, I'm over playing records, a few of them the same as we have at home. I get a big kick out of doing this because it reminds me of the nights we all used to sit around the Victrola and listen for hours at a time *(It reminds me that, 6 years later, he will begin his lifelong career as a broadcaster & will become a well-known DC, later Philadelphia, DJ)*. You better stock up on needles 'cause when I get home, I will probably wear that thing out.

Say, I wish you'd tell our mess sergeant how to make lemon pie. We were served some today that tasted like glue. No foolin', I've said it before and I'll say it again: you make the world's best lemon pie.

Oh, before I forget; please tell Pop that I still have the ten-dollar bill he loaned me in Union Station the day I left and I'll mail it to him as soon as I can. Don't worry, I didn't spend it. I turned it in to the battalion officer along with my watch for safe keeping. I'll be able to obtain it right before I leave Parris Island. The reason I turned my watch in for safe keeping is because of the sand around here. It ruins nearly all watches no matter how good they are. Some fellows didn't deposit theirs, and now the sand has stopped some and caused others to keep faulty time. I'll be able to use it at Camp Lejeune, though.

Say, could you send me a couple of handkerchiefs? I brought 2 with me. One was lost on the train and the other is pretty tattered. And could you please induce Pat to whip up a little batch of her super-delicious fudge and send it down sometime? Gosh, I must sound like a parasite. Troublesome gremlin, ain't I?

And for that special note for the gremlin of the household (slight pause for note to "Runt"):

Dear "Runt",

Gosh, I miss you, you little squirt. Did the Easter bunny come to see you? I wrote him a letter and told him to be sure and leave plenty of eggs for my Bonnie. You be a good girl now and spank your big sister and your Daddy every night, and take good care of your Mama. Tell *(neighbors)* Charlie Carter and Carter hello for me. So long for now. See ya' soon.
Love, Bunk

Taps are in a few minutes, so I better quit for now. I'll write again as soon as possible.
Love to all, Bunk

P.S. Thanks a lot for the Digest and the book of cartoons. I really got a kick out of them.

****

(*Parris Island S.C.*)
(*Sun.*) April 22, 1945

Dear Mother,

I guess there's been an inexcusable space between this and my last letter. Again, the only reason, and a threadbare one at that, I have to offer is being kept busy. I bet you're getting pretty fed up with that one. I promise to be more regular from now on. We have just completed our final week of training on the rifle range. During this past week, we have been marched from one part of the range to the other, throwing grenades and firing several kinds of rifles. We haven't even had time to wash our hands before chow. Boy, what a delicious combination: beef stew mixed with powder stains, rifle oil and target paste off your hands!

Also, this week we fired the M-1 rifle (that's the regular Garand) and the Browning Automatic Rifle for a final score to determine our ratings with these weapons. I earned a silver marksman's bar with the rifle and a sharpshooter's rating with the B.A.R. Last night, we started our mess duty. It's not hard, but somewhat monotonous. We have to get up about 3 or 3:30 A.M. Oh, well, we only have two weeks of this, and then our final week of training, which means, as far as I know, only three more weeks on Parris Island. We then shove off for Camp Lejeune and are there about three days before leaving on furlough. I should be home about the last week of May, maybe sooner, who knows?

I heard from (*Cousins*) Sud and Din yesterday. Sud says that I will be close enough at Camp Lejeune to see him on weekends. Boy, that'd be swell. As you know, Dinny has been transferred to someplace in Texas temporarily. He said it's as isolated as Siberia. It rains there one day, freezes the next, and then turns hot as blazes. Some joint, eh? I also got a nice long letter from (*Uncle*) Pete. It sure was swell to hear from him. He says he thinks that he'll be shipped right to the Pacific when the mess in Europe is over. That sure is a dirty dig, because if anyone deserves to get home, Pete certainly does. (*Pete, Nat's youngest uncle, was brilliant, majored in pre-med &, before he was drafted, had been accepted by Johns Hopkins for medical school. He was older than most draftees. His brilliance & education were ignored, & he ended up in an Army motor pool, repairing truck motors.*)

Boy, did I get a surprise the other night. I was sweeping in front of the barracks, when suddenly from the barracks next door, I heard a mellow trombone blast forth. I quickly recognized it but I thought I must be wacky or something. So I raced next door and, sure enough, it was (*High school buddy*) Willie Hetrick He had just gotten in from

Camp Lejeune and had come around looking for me. He somehow got in the wrong barracks, where one fellow had a trombone. So Willie proceeded to give out with a solo. Boy, was I glad to see him! He has completed his training at Camp Lejeune and has been transferred to the band.

I also ran into Billy Durham, who used to go to Anacostia. He is taking his boot training here in platoon 129. I was sure surprised to see him. *(Nat has told me that his nickname was, naturally, "Bull".)*

Oh, by the way, I've been confirmed and my name has been sent to St. Timothy's Chapel *(in D.C.)* for enrollment. I don't know too much about the Episcopal Church but I am learning as I go along. Imagine me, the family heathen, being confirmed!

Roosevelt's death came as a kick in the pants to us down here. Regardless of party prejudices, most of the fellows agreed that he was the man best qualified to lead us out of this mess. Nobody is very much elated over the prospect of Truman taking the helm. *(Nat did a turn-around of this view later in life. He concluded that my cousin Harry Truman had been an excellent leader & he became quite a Truman scholar.)* But, as you said, we've all got to back him in order to make a success of our war campaign.

Tell Pat thanks for the fudge. It was really swell. I'll answer her letter as soon as I can.

We've gotta go over and get the chow hall ready for evening chow in a few minutes, so I better quit for now. More later.

Love, Bunk

P.S. Tell the "Runt" I miss her and to make her old man eat his spinach and chocolate pudding.   Bunk

****

(A birthday letter to sister Bonnie.)

(Parris Island S.C.)
(Wed.) April 25,1945

Dear "Runt",

By the time you get this you probably will be five years old. Gosh, I wish I could be with you on your birthday, but maybe I can make it next year. Just think, Runt, five at last! When I was home, you were always telling me about the wonderful things that are going to happen when you are five. I sure hope they all come true. It's hard to believe that you are getting to be a big girl now. It seems like only last week that you were a roly-poly, curly-headed little squirt who used to crawl around saying "tee" and "dook" *("see" & "look")*. But pretty soon you'll be starting to school. I'm sure thankful that I've got a little sister here in this country where a little girl can go to a good school, play in a safe street, and go to sleep at night without being afraid. It's always got to be that way. That's why I'm down here instead of home with you on your birthday ~ to help make sure it stays that way. I'm sorry I can't send you a present. (There's nothing here that five-year-olds would like.) Let's hope I can deliver a nice, big present in person on your next birthday. Well, so long, five-year-old. Have a big day - a happy birthday, Bonnie.

Love, Bunk

****

Parris Island, S.C.)
(Sat.) May 12, 1945

Dear Mother,

Boot camp is almost over. Today is our last training day. We will be here Sunday and Monday and will leave early Tuesday morning for Camp Lejeune. We'll be there about three days and then, home! Gosh, that'll sure be a wonderful 10 days! *(Nat never again mentions the 10-day furlough. He had it & quite a few weekend liberties.)*

I've started this letter twice, on Tuesday and today. We've been kept on the run so much during our final week of training that, by Wednesday, I was only half-way through the one I had started early last Tuesday. So I decided to make another attempt at a more timely letter today.

We got back from the rifle range last Saturday after four weeks of training and two weeks of mess duty out there. During the mess duty, I had to wait on the non-commissioned officers' table. I had to act just like a head-waiter in a French restaurant because NCOs are pretty particular people. The mess sergeant called me "Tarzan", because I'm such a "big boy", of course (Heh! Heh!).

I don't know how, but I somehow earned a sharpshooter's rating with the Browning Automatic Rifle. You should have seen me firing the thing. It weighs 21 lbs. and every time I pressed the trigger and fired, it pulled me forward on the ground. This really tickled my coaches. One of them laughed and yelled, "Hey, boy. Who the hell told you to advance? Git on back there! Ya tryin' to win the war by yourself?"

Gosh, I'm sorry this letter will be late for Mother's Day, but this is the first chance I've had to write a full letter this week. I haven't had a chance to mail a remembrance of some sort, but I'll bring a nice big one when I come home. I'll be thinking of you on Mother's Day, anyway, and wishing like everything that I could be with you. So have a happy day on me.

Say, do you remember a boy by the name of Albert Daisley? He went to school with me in the second grade in Baltimore. I ran into him down here. Boy, has he gotten big.

Durn, there were so many people I wanted and should have written to, but never could seem to find time to write to all of them. I'll save my apologies till I get home.

I really got a kick out of hearing about the Cadets winning battalion drill. I would've given my eye teeth to have been there. The High School Cadets is one of the finest organizations there is. The years I spent as a member were some of the most valuable of my life. I had a heck of a lot of fun too.

Well, I gotta run now. I'll write next time probably from Camp Lejeune. See ya' soon.

Love, Bunk

****

(*Camp Lejeune, N.C.*)
(*Tue.*) June 3, 1945

Dear Mother,

I've been at Camp Lejeune for about a week now and this is the first chance I've had to write. We've been assigned to quarters and have been issued our gear, such as rifle, helmet, etc. Our company has already been on a couple of hikes. They keep us on the go during the day, but the nights are ours to spend as we please. However, during the last week, our free time at night has been taken up by training films, inspections and what-not. This only happens maybe one week out of two or three. However, next week we are scheduled for a couple of night marches. Now that I'm more familiar with the set-up, I feel pretty sure I can space my time so as to be able to write more often.

Oh, say! We had a training film on map-reading the other night and they showed a map of the upper Potomac region which included Washington and vicinity. On the map they also showed Oxon Run, Suitland (*Despite their DC address, Nat's family lived in Suitland MD*), Silver Hill and Upper Marlboro. I nearly jumped out of my seat.

This sure is a big place: over 70 square miles, I hear (No one seems to really know). It is made up mostly of vast wooded areas and wide fields. There are maneuver areas. There are several posts or settlements situated at various points about the camp. First of all there is Tent City where I am quartered. This is where fellows taking combat training are quartered in a group of tents and prefabricated huts. I live in one of the huts. The durn thing leaks like a sieve when it rains. In fact, I have often contemplated moving outside. It certainly can't be any wetter. Some of the other posts are Hadnot Point (camp headquarters), the Naval Hospital, the BAM's boot camp, Trailer Camp and Onslow's Beach. These posts are scattered at various points about the camp and require a bus service between them (at least that's what they tell me. Any place I ever went in camp, I "hoofed" it). There are a couple of air strips here, too.

We have a pretty nice recreation hall containing pool and ping pong tables, magazine racks, bowling games, a piano and a Victrola. There's also a swell camp theatre showing <u>free</u> movies. (Don't tell (*High school friend*) Jerry or he might fly down). We have a pretty good PX, too. We can use these facilities any time during our spare time.

How's everybody up there? I hope the "Runt's" tonsils haven't acted up any more. Say, please let me know how Anacostia Cadets do in competitive drill. The competition is this coming Thursday and

Friday. Tell Hugh I think A Co. has <u>second</u> place sewed up (B Co.'ll be first, "natch").

I'm fairly sure of getting weekend liberty next week. If so, I can be home for Sunday. If I can get home, I'll wire you either Friday night or Saturday. Weekend liberty extends from Saturday afternoon to reveille Monday morning. So be on the lookout for me.

I gotta wash out some dirty dungarees now, so, so-long for now.

Love to all, Bunk

P.S. Please send me *(high school friends)* Dick Murphy's and Bill Huff's addresses. They are written down somewhere around the house.

＊＊＊＊

(Camp Lejeune, N.C.)
Sun. June 24, '45

Dear Mother,

At last a word from your wandering son! I've done quite a bit of tramping since you last saw me. I got back into camp at 3:30 Monday morning. *(after a weekend liberty)* Reveille came at 5:00 AM and at 7:30 AM we shoved off on a 12-mile hike. Oh, was I groggy! I was walking in my sleep for the first five miles. We were toting 80-lb. packs and I was carrying a Browning Automatic Rifle besides. We set up our bivouac in some God-forgotten pine grove, put up tents, and dug fox holes. By the time taps rolled around, I felt like a dehydrated hangover (dad-ratted PX pen).

We spent a week out there, learning platoon, squad and fire team tactics. They fed us K and C rations. They weren't bad but they got kinda' monotonous. These rations were made up of usually a small can of cheese or some kind of meat preparation and several small packets containing powdered coffee, chewing gum, candy and some wafers re-sembling dog biscuits. Not that those "dog biscuits" had much effect on me, but sometimes (arf! arf!) I don't (arf! arf!) feel quite (arf!) myself. All in all, it was pretty interesting and I liked it O.K. The rub was the trek out and back. We were a pretty tired bunch when we got back Saturday noon. The mail didn't reach us till Friday afternoon. I re-ceived then the letter you wrote Monday night. I would have answered it but we spent the majority of our time crawling around like a bunch of banshees.

Willie Hetrick is now stationed at Tent City. He dropped around to see me last night. He's quartered a few blocks away from me. It'll be swell to be able to see him often!

Gosh, I enjoyed last Sunday. They were the swellest eight hours I ever spent. *(He was obviously home on weekend liberty, which gave him only one day at home, the rest of the time on a bus.)* I feel pretty sure I will be able to make it again soon. If so, I'll phone you long distance from camp early on the Saturday before I get home. Phone connections from camp are pretty good, so anytime I get a chance, you should have at least 18 hours notice before I get home. I wish I could give you more advance notice, but a guy can't even accurately predict tomorrow around here, things are that uncertain.

18-year-old fellows are expected to start a third phase of training in about two weeks. This will take place here at Camp Lejeune and should last about a month. During this phase, I'll get more bivouac, some training in machine guns and mortars and training in amphibious landings.

Now listen here! I don't want you to worry one bit. I'm getting the best training in the world and I'm with a swell bunch of fellows. There's at least one good laugh every day, and no matter how tough things get, I'll be content as long as there's at least one hearty belly laugh each day. Nonsensical philosophy, eh what? Oh well, I always was screwy that way.

It's getting on, so I better quit for now. Tell Pat I'll write very soon.
Love to all, Bunk

P.S. Please send the last edition of the Pow-Wow. *(Nat's Anacostia High School newspaper, to which he had been a regular contributor of articles & cartoons.)*

****

5 POSTCARDS *(Addressed by Nat's mother to herself. Probably given to Nat on one of his liberties home. All from Lejeune. It was an unsuccessful experiment, as postcards did not accommodate his narrative letter-writing style. He wrote all 5 cards before mailing them all at once!)*

(Thu.) June 28 *(1945)*

Dear Mother,

Well, we've been back from bivouac almost a week now and my feet still feel like pontoons. Solid food sure tastes good after K rations. Today we were taught village warfare by attacking a life-size model of a Jap village known as "Little Tokyo". It rained clinkers, so our NCOs took us inside one of the buildings and they started a roaring crap game. (Don't worry, I crawled in a corner and slept all through the game).

Love, Bunk

(Sat.) June 30 *(1945)*

Dear Mother,

I'm writing this before breakfast and as you can probably tell by the writing, I'm still half asleep. My name was on the list of ones to get weekend liberty, but all liberties have been cancelled as our company goes on regimental guard duty this week-end. Oh, well, maybe next week-end I'll see you. If so I'll be sure and notify you ahead of time.

Love, Bunk

(Sun.) July 1 *(1945)*

Dear Mother,

Had a little time between guard watches so I dropped around to see Willie Hetrick and Billy Durham. Both are stationed here at Tent City. It sure is swell to see some old school pals here. I helped lower the colors last night and post them this morning. I sure got a big kick out of it. Am gonna be relieved in a little while, then to bed.

Love, Bunk

(Wed.) July 4 *(1945)*

Dear Mother,

Today I really celebrated the 4th with some real fireworks. I went to the dentist's!! Oh my sad jaw! I only had a couple of cavities but it felt like a mouthful. I ran into Al Daisley, my old Baltimore chum. He was also on his way to the dentist's. Lucky boy! Say, do you think you could possibly dig up a copy of the last issue of the *(High school paper)* Pow Wow and send it down?

Love, Bunk

(Thu.) July 5 *(1945)*

Dear Mother,

You'll probably get all my previous cards at once because, after writing each one, I placed it in a small box in the top of my sea bag intending to mail it later and I plumb forgot about it. This happened several times and I eventually accumulated quite a collection so I'm sending them all out with this one. Oh well, at least you'll get all the news in one lump. Am feeling swell and hope you all are the same.

Love, Bunk

****

(Camp Lejeune, N.C.)
(Sun.) July 15, 1945

Dear Pat,

I can hear the clinkers hitting the fan as a result, no doubt, of receiving an immense shock caused by getting a letter from your illiterate brother. The gap in my correspondence was caused by moving to a new battalion. We were told to make up a transport pack and to pack our sea bags and stand by for transfer. Everybody was pretty excited, as we heard rumors about going to this place and that and fellows were making bets as to where we would end up. At any rate, we were expecting to be traveling a pretty good distance. Well, after all the preparation, suspense, etc., we finally wound up in a new battalion, just two blocks away from our old one!!! My new address, as you can see by the envelope, is practically the same as my old one, except that I'm now in Co. C, 3rd TRNG. BN., 2nd PLT. The rest of my address is the same as before.

Last weekend, I took off for Jacksonville on a week-end pass hoping to catch a bus for D.C.

However, the line was so long that I wouldn't have been able to get a bus until after 9 P.M. and that would have been too late. So I went instead to Wilmington, a small coastal city about 50 miles away. First we, Paul Leclair from Canada and myself, went to a U.S.O. dance, but the girls were older and incidentally, taller than us, so we went to the roller rink. That was more like it (WOOF! WOOF!)!! The girls there were /////// (oops! Censored! Musta thought I was writing to Jerry), to continue, smaller and more - uh — well, you know kinda' - sorta' -

- see what I mean?

You know me on roller skates, as graceful as Lil' Abner dancing on ping pong balls in a china shop. However, my awkwardness came in very handy as I clipped more good lookers that way (Some clip joint!). The manager of the joint said it was incredible how I managed to be all over the floor at once. However (some day I'll learn a synonym for that word), I explained that a Marine is trained to land on a position and cover it with his entire flank (and as you know, I'm pretty well equipped for any job involving "the flanks"). I ran into (literally) a very nice girl, small (about the size of "Shortie" Foster from Centerville), and very nice looking. After the rink closed, Paul, the fellow who came with me, and I left for Carolina Beach.

This is a summer resort about 12 miles from Wilmington. It's sort of a miniature Atlantic City with a small boardwalk, a few ferris wheels, merry-go-rounds, bath houses, hot dog stands, penny arcades, shooting galleries, etc. and a long, wide beach. We hit there about 1 A.M. Sunday morning and went to a rooming house where Paul had phoned in a reservation Saturday afternoon when we left Jacksonville. But when we arrived there, we found that we were too late and the landlady had turned our room over to 5 members of a swing band who had come to play for a dance that day.

Paul and I went up to find out what the story was. We banged on the door and when it opened, I nearly dropped a truckload of "you-know-whats", for two of the fellows in the band turned out to be none other than *(high school buddies)* John Stevens and Spencer Sinatra *(A musically talented relative of Frank Sinatra. Nat told me that Spencer strongly resembled Frank).* I sure got a big kick out of seeing them. I talked with them for over two hours. Then Paul and I went in search of sleeping quarters. We couldn't stay with the bandsmen because they were overcrowded as it was. So we eventually ended up obtaining a blanket from a bath house and sleeping on the beach. The mosquitoes chewed us up and we woke up with the tide around our feet, but other than that, we didn't make out so bad. After we woke up, we spent the rest of the day swimming and eating hot dogs, etc. Sure had fun, but I'd still rather have spent the week end home (nine hours of it, anyway).

On our way back to Camp Lejeune, I bought a watermelon in Wilmington. Paul was too tired to eat any, but not me; so I ravenously devoured the whole works right in the middle of the sidewalk. Sure was good!

For the past week we have been on bivouac. We have two more weeks coming. Oh, brethren and sistren!! You see, we have begun our 3rd phase of training, lasting five weeks, three of which are spent on bivouac. They feed us like birds (humming birds at that) on bivouac. Do you think "you all" could send "me all" a box of either candy or cookies, could 'ja, huh? Could 'ja, huh? Could 'ja, huh?

I haven't heard from my overseas physical yet, but I don't expect to for a while yet (ran out of ink).

I sure was sorry to hear about *(Cousin)* Bill's foot injury. It really happened at a tough time, just when the good money was coming in. Oh, well, maybe now he'll take a rest. He works too hard anyway. Let me know if *(Cousin)* Dinny transfers. I'm gonna write him and *(Cousin)* Sud each a long letter. Tell Mother and Aunt Sis thanks for their letters and I'll write soon.

Love, Nat

P.S. Am enclosing a picture taken at the beach.

****

(This letter was worth saving just for the realization that many of these Marines were still boys & acted accordingly!)

(Camp Lejeune, N.C.)
(Tue.) July 24, 1945

Dear Mother,

Long time no hear. I guess that old saying (All right, maybe I did twist it a little) holds true in regard to the large gap in my correspondence home. Well, right after I sent you a card notifying you of my change of address, we shoved off on a two weeks' bivouac. It sure threw me way behind in my letter writing. We got back Saturday, so put down the hair brush, Momma, I'll be more regular from now on. I'm now on guard duty.

We didn't go out quite as far as our first trip, but far enough, thanks. It rained almost incessantly the whole time we were out there. That's the longest shower I ever took. I was soaked to the hide most all the time.

We had fun one day. Our platoon had to dig foxholes in the rain. As I dug deeper into the ground, I noticed that my foxhole was beginning to resemble a bath tub as I found myself waist-deep in water. However, most of the others were in the same fix. So we figured as long as we were wet, we may as well enjoy ourselves. The result was a royal mud battle. Mud and what-not was flying thick and fast when our corporal intervened, only to be pelted with a very gooey clod. I never saw a bunch of heads duck down into foxholes so fast before in my life.

We were supposed to have another week of bivouac besides the two we completed, but they cancelled it. I don't think anyone was disappointed. However, we may get that extra week later on. We're supposed to get over a month more of training here at Camp Lejeune so don't worry, I'll be around a while yet.

Willie Hetrick is now on the west coast. I got a nice letter from his mother. She's helping Willie and me to keep tabs on each other. Have the Murphys heard from Dick?

I had my ticket and was all set to shove off for D.C. when something came up. I was called into the top kick's office and told that I had to be at the dental clinic at 7:00 P.M. Sat. night. Well, there was my weekend shot right there. I had two jaw teeth pulled by a very suave dentist who persisted in humming, "The Yanks are coming". Oh, well, I'm still livin'. I'm gonna get up there some weekend or bust. I'll probably bring my bunk mate, Sneezy Snyder, with me. He's really a swell egg.

Two letters that I wrote to *(Cousin)* Sud at Duke were returned. I'm gonna write to him at Great Lakes as soon as I finish this. Has *(Cousin)* Dinny been transferred or is he still at Amarillo? I lost his address when I changed to this battalion. Could you send it to me? I was sorry to hear that *(Cousin)* Bill couldn't get into the Navy. Maybe he can get what he wants through the draft. *(Bill had been excused from military service as the only 1 of 3 sons left available to help on the farm & he desperately wanted to join the military.)*

Hope everyone is fine up there.

Love to you all, Bunk

****

(This letter and the next 6 were written on Camp Lejeune letterhead, white with a black scene of Marines in battle gear coming ashore on a beach out of landing craft, weapons at the ready. Planes are above them, two hit, on fire & on their way into the sea. Enough to make a mother have nightmares! The war still raged, though Japanese surrender was expected imminently. Nat was in the Lejeune Field Hospital during this time because the NCO in charge of training maneuvers forced him to crawl or dig through poison ivy during foxhole training … "It's just a bunch of weeds, Chick." When Nat contracted it, poison ivy was a worst-case scenario. He had nearly died of a case of it a couple of years earlier, fighting a forest fire with his cousins on the Eastern Shore. A new drug, sulfa, obtained by his country doctor from a friend at Annapolis Naval Station across the Bay, saved his life that time. I killed acres of it in my lifetime with Nat, to protect him from it. This letter was almost destroyed by frequent reading. Also, it is obvious that these letters were mailed in too-small envelopes & that he had a bad time folding them with his poison-ivy hands. They were difficult to smooth out enough to make them readable & are falling apart.)

(Camp Lejeune Field Hospital)
Sun. Aug. 5, 1945

Dear Mother,

It looks like I'm going back to my bad habits again, being tardy with my letter writing. This time my excuse is due to my old nemesis, poison ivy. As you can probably tell by my handwriting, I have it on my hands, but completely! Today is the first time I have been able to grip a pencil. I got the stuff Tuesday digging a foxhole and, by taps that night, it had started to raise up. When I got up Wednesday morning I had a couple of blisters the size of golf balls. For the next day or so, Sneezy had to tie my shoes, tuck my shirt tail in for me, and other things here and there, as my hands were pretty useless. He told me, "Boy, after the way I've babied you, you better remember me on Mother's Day." The stuff kept gettin' worse so they sent me to the field hospital for treatment. Now don't get worried! I've been here a couple days and all I do is lay around reading magazines and once in a while I soak my hands in some sort of solution. I'm getting along fine and should be out of the hospital in a couple of days.

My battalion leaves tomorrow morning for Onslow Beach for a week of amphibious training. Sneezy says if I miss it because of being in the hospital, he's gonna bring back a helmet-load of salt water and pour it over my head.

Have you heard anything from *(Uncle)* Pete as to when he'll be home? I sure hope he can make it soon. If anybody has a right to be homesick, he does.

It's time for me to soak my hands again, so I'd better sign off for now. There's really nothing much to this hospital life. Nothin' much happens, except I'm getting enough sleep to last me the whole war.

Hope everybody's fine.

Love to all, Bunk

P.S. I ran into a fellow whose last name is Barnes who lives in Baltimore and knows *(Cousins)* Peggy and Dinny and the Whitimores *(family friends)*. He went to Poly. He's in my company.

****

(Camp Lejeune Field Hospital)
Tues. Aug. 7 *(1945)*

Dear Mother,

Nothing much doing around these diggins. In the hospital, you don't live, you just exist. Time stands still here. I had to think twice before I knew what day it was.

My hands are clearing up pretty fast. I can use them better now. There are fellows in this ward with everything from elephantiasis and measles to poison ivy.

(Cousin) Dinny's birthday is Saturday. Could you send me his address? I lost it in transferring battalions. Yours comes up Monday. Wish I could send you something but right now I'm caught kinda short. You see, we get paid on the 5th and 20th of each month. I was here in the hospital on the 5th and I missed being paid. So I'll collect the whole works on the 20th, which is just a short time off, so I'll make out. I'm not eligible for liberty this weekend, anyway.

I've tried all the PXs in Tent City, but none as yet have gotten in any more of those pins. I'll keep trying, though.

The chow's being brought in, so I better get it while the "gittin's" good.

Love to all, Bunk

****

(Camp Lejeune Field Hospital)
Wed. Aug. 8 *(1945)*

Dear Mother,

I received your box of chocolates today. Thanks heaps. Sure were swell. And when I say were, I mean definitely past tense, as they were almost totally devoured, the moment I got the wrapper off, by a bunch of wolves who call themselves my ward mates. However, I managed to hold on to a few. Really are delicious.

The blisters have gone down and the stuff is steadily drying up. And doggoned if I'm not gaining weight due to this diet of concentrated loafing.

I know this is awful short but in this place, activity is just non-existent. In short there just ain't nothing to tell. So, till tomorrow,

Love to all, Bunk

P.S. I took a bath in a real honest to gosh tub today.

****

(Camp Lejeune Field Hospital)
Fri. Aug. 10 *(1945)*

Dear Mother,

Here it is Friday and I'm still in this dad-ratted hospital. My hands have practically all cleared up except for one spot on my right hand and that is kinda' slow. I feel swell and am gettin' fat and lazy.

At long last the Pow-Wow arrived today. I sure was glad to get it. Had a swell time getting caught up on stuff that happened at school. Say, did you notice George Kennedy's letter in the Pow-Wow?

Oh, by the way, even though I'm in the hospital, my mail is sent to my regular address and they forward it to me. So just use my regular address.

'Nuff said for now ,
Love, Bunk

****

(Camp Lejeune Field Hospital)
Sat., Aug. 11 *(1945)*

Dear Mother,

Uh-huh, I'm still confined in the "Inner Sanctum". The doctor says I'll be here a couple days yet. I shouldn't beef, as this is what might be called the life of Riley, but even Riley gets restless, I'll bet.

Got a letter from Pat. From what she says, it must be pretty wet up there. It was pretty rainy here for a while, but lately we've hit a stretch of good weather. I sure hope it continues, for the sake of my company who's camping at Onslow Beach. I'd sure liked to have been at *(Cousin)* Bill's party. I sure miss the farm gang.

I'm writing this while sitting outside the front door of our ward. The sun has just gone down and the mosquitoes are determined to drive me indoors so I'll quit for now.
Love to all, Bunk

****

Mon., Aug. 13, 1945
(Camp Lejeune Field Hospital)

Dear Mother,

OR, IF YOU"D PREFER IT IN VERSE:

Even though down here I be
Far away from old D.C.
I pause to shout herewith, comma,
Happy birthday to my Momma.   *Bunk*

I sure wish I could be with you on your birthday. Maybe next year, huh? We get paid next Monday, so I'll send you something then.

My hands have practically all cleared up so I should be out of the hospital in a day or two. I feel fine.

That's all for now. Am thinking of you.

Love to all,
Bunk

P.S. Sneezy says many happy returns.

P.P.S. Maybe the war'll be over tomorrow. That'd be a pretty swell birthday present.

Bunk

****

*(Like the 6 previous letters from the hospital, but this one was written on **VJ Day!** What a special letter for a guy who was expecting to ship out to invade Japan within weeks. This letter is the most-read of the batch. It is very fragile)*

(Camp Lejeune Field Hospital)
Tues., Aug. 14, 1945

Dear Mother,

It's over at last, and now you and Aunt Fanny and Aunt Sis and countless other mothers can at last relax and breathe a long-awaited sigh of relief. Yours has been the toughest part of this war. There's nothing worse than waiting, worrying and uncertainty, and that's the part you've been forced to play. So now the dirty business is over with, thank God, and you can take it easy.

Luckily, we somehow obtained a radio in our ward and we tuned in on Truman's announcement of the Japanese surrender. Later we heard Prime Minister Atlee's speech from London. But the best program of all was broadcast directly from 16th & Penna. Ave. N.W. in front of the White House. Boy, you shoulda' heard the whoopin' and hollerin' of the crowd *(She probably did, at least on the radio)*. I joined right in with 'em till one of my fellow inmates clouted me with a bedpan and said emphatically as follows: **"SHADDUP!!!"**

I can just picture me in 40 years with a grandchild on each knee. They'll look up at me and say, "Grandpap, what did you do in the war?" And I'll proudly stroke my beard and say, "Well, brats, when the war ended I was in the hospital at Camp Lejeune fighting the battle of poison ivy." Fine war!!! (Ah's regusted).

Oh, by the way, I just looked in the top drawer of my foot locker and found a letter that I wrote to you yesterday *(the birthday card!)* but forgot to mail, so you'll probably get it along with this one.

I guess there are a lot of happy guys writing home tonight. Peace is at last here. God, I hope it sticks this time.

'Nuff for now,
Love to all, Bunk

P.S. I just watched the sun set. I guess it's about the prettiest sunset this world has seen for quite a while.

(I found this letter so touching, as this 18-year-old concentrated on what the Japanese surrender meant to the mothers of the fighting men, rather than to himself. His comment about the sunset further shows his tender side.)

****

(This description of Nat's troop train journey across the U.S. is amazing. It covered both sides of 9 sheets of stationery. He can't have taken notes. He always wished to repeat that trip. I wish he [or we] had done that.)

(Camp Pendleton CA)
Fri. Aug. 31, 1945

Dear Mother,

Well, at long last here I am in California. Our troop train pulled into Camp Pendleton at around 6:30 last night, after a 5 day trip across country. We have been placed in barracks up in the mountains of Southern California. We are about 37 miles from San Diego and 86 miles from Los Angeles *(Nat was a history, geography & current events enthusiast from his earliest school years. Map study was a lifelong passion with him).* I also found out that I'm only 64 miles from Long Beach, where Bob James *(A school friend)* lives now. The nearest town is Oceanside, about the size of Easton, Md., 10 miles away. There's right much to see out here, but I don't expect to be here long enough to see much.

I wish I could adequately describe my trip across country. As I had seldom in my life ever been out of the Baltimore-Washington-Eastern Shore triangle, you can imagine what a kick I got out of it. We took the southern route through the Carolinas, Georgia, Alabama, Mississippi, Louisiana, Texas, New Mexico, Arizona and southern California. The train pulled out of Camp Lejeune Saturday afternoon August 25.

I was in a way glad to leave that place. We had been there so long that we were starting to repeat some training and, besides, it had been raining almost incessantly since July 10 and the joint was extremely muddy. Of course it meant no more weekends at home. That was the main rub of leaving Camp Lejeune. But even so, I was pretty lucky to get home those weekends. *(Cousin)* Dinny has been in the service 3 weeks longer than I have and he's never even been near home. It may not be very long before Dinny, *(Cousin)* Sud, *(Uncle)* Pete and all of us will be back home together.

Anyhow, we pulled out of Camp Lejeune Saturday afternoon, the 25th. We slept in Pullmans, two to a berth, but not too crowded. I woke up the next morning, Sunday the 26th in South Carolina. It was different than North Carolina. There were rolling green hills very much like the ones between D.C. and Annapolis. By late morning we were passing through the northwestern part of Georgia. This was the first part of the trip that really impressed me. This section was made up of incredibly high, steep hills with real, honest-to-gosh log cabins perched precariously on the crests and slopes. Running between the ridges were pretty, green valley floors covered with corn, melon patches and fruit orchards. *(This farm boy knew his crops at a glance.)* This looked like real "Lil' Abner" country. We pulled into Atlanta at noon. I couldn't see much of that town except freight yards.

At about two o'clock that afternoon we crossed into Alabama. As we went through mostly the northern part until late that night, I didn't see a single cotton field in Alabama. Northern Alabama was very similar to northwestern Georgia except the hills were rockier and there were no orchards to speak of. We got into Birmingham at about 6 P.M. and got off for a few minutes of calisthenics. This place looked an awful lot like Baltimore, except that most everybody had either hogs or chickens in their back yards. I slept right through Mississippi.

On Mon. morning, August 27, I woke up in New Orleans. I've never seen any place like it. It's like being in a foreign city. As we hit the outskirts, we saw attractive white cottages and rose bushes galore. Then, as we got farther in, we came across narrow streets and quaint houses, of French and Spanish type architecture. I also noticed quite a few colored women balancing baskets on their heads. Then, as the train went out the other side, we saw wide, green parks and palm trees. I also got a fleeting glimpse of the Tulane Sugar Bowl stadium. Someday I'd like to go back and really see New Orleans.

We then turned north and went up past Louisiana State University (some joint) to Baton Rouge, where we crossed over the Mississippi River on a barge. It sure is a distinguished looking body of water, very muddy though. However, I saw a lot of those old-time river steamers you read about. In Louisiana I saw a lot of sugar cane fields and low, swampy bayous covered with leafy lily-pads. There were crane and swan all over the place. We entered Texas about 9:00 P.M. that night.

We pulled into Beaumont, Texas at around 10:00 P.M., and the weather took a turn for the worse. By the time we got to Houston we had come into a hurricane zone. The train rocked some for a while, but by morning we were out of the storm area. Almost all the next day we traveled past large farms, made up made up mostly of vast cotton, corn and pasture fields. We then came into the Texas prairie. It's hard to believe anything could be as vast and wide as that prairie. At one point we could see a city almost 25 miles off in the distance. Gradually the trees became smaller and scrubbier looking as we hit cattle country (didn't see any cowboys, durn it!). At Temple, Texas, we got off for calisthenics. Later we hit the red-clay badlands, covered with sparse, greenish purple sagebrush. Blue, table-top ridges began rising here and there. By this time the sun was setting and it sure was beautiful. At about 3:00 A.M. Wednesday morning the 29th, we crossed into New Mexico, in my opinion, the most picturesque state we went through.

First we crossed rolling green plains much like north-central Texas, but soon the land became sandier and dry-looking and there was a lot of sage. Then we came to a range of rocky, table-top ridges, similar to the ones in Texas, but higher, rockier and clay-colored instead of blue. Around 9:30 A.M. we entered one of the prettiest little valleys I've ever seen; a long, narrow, fertile valley bounded on one side by high, misty-blue peaks and, on the other side, by a shelf of red-clay table land. It was made up of small farms growing mostly wheat and corn.

We passed some small pastures with dairy herds being tended by Mexicans wearing big sombreros. There were also quite a few Indians working in the corn fields. Right in the middle of the valley is the town of Belin, New Mexico, inhabited mostly by Mexicans and Indians. Soon we were riding through the red table land again and it was along here that I saw countless clay adobe huts *(Nat could not have dreamed then that he would eventually be privileged to have an artistically talented Native American son-in-law who would present his in-laws with his beautiful painting of one of these adobe houses!)*. We passed several Pueblo villages and many Indians were still living in the cliffs like their ancestors. It was really impressive. We crossed the Arizona line that afternoon.

Arizona was very similar to New Mexico except that there were more Indians. It didn't strike me as being as pretty as New Mexico either. We passed a lot of trading posts selling Indian goods.

There were also quite a few dude ranches. I saw a lot of beautiful horses (but hardly any girls, durn it!). However, we did pass some tourist camps near Flagstaff, Arizona, where there were some pip lookin' babes and, true to tradition, the whole train proceeded to holler, howl, whistle, etc. out of the windows. One guy leaned out of the window so far he nearly got tangled up with a passing freight (One of my buddies held on to my feet, though). We started coming into the mountains at Flagstaff. Here our officers and N.C.O.s took on a load of everything from corn whiskey to California wine. A sergeant and corporal staggered right off the train but we stopped to pick them up. None of the privates had anything to drink. (I can't grow on that stuff anyhow.) In western Arizona we passed through some pretty green valleys with tall cedars. I was on guard that night when we crossed the Colorado River into California at 2:23 A.M. (Pacific Post-war time) Aug. 30th.

When I woke up Thursday morning, we were crossing the desert. The desert consisted of a seemingly endless stretch of rocky, sandy, level land sparsely covered with clumps of dry, brown brush and bounded on either side by distant blue ridges. We got off for more calisthenics at Barstow, California. Between Barstow and San Bernardino *(They were following Route 66!)*, we passed dry-looking hills on which grew brown grass and tree-like cactus plants. Just before we hit San Bernardino, we saw some of the loftiest peaks that we came across on our whole trip. While passing through San Bernardino and practically all the rest of the way to Camp Pendleton, we saw countless orange and lemon groves, some so close we could almost reach out the window and grab some. Some places the people threw oranges to us (or at us, I don't know which). I also saw a lot of oil wells. They throw 'em up everywhere out here, some even in the middle of orange groves. The train then headed right down along the Pacific Coast. We were only about 50 yards from the ocean at some points. After while, we turned off into the mountains and finally debarked at Pendleton.

I probably won't be able to mail this for a few days as they haven't given us a return address yet. We expect to ship overseas very soon, but maybe I'll get to see some of "Chloroformia".

Did you get the bracelet I sent you.? Sorry I couldn't dig up a pin like your old one.

As soon as I learn the layout of things, I'll try to contact you by phone or wire or something. At any rate, you should hear from me one way or the other before you receive this.

Almost taps so I better quit for now.

Love to all, Bunk

P.S. Sneezy and I got separated, durn it!! He's probably in some barracks nearby so maybe I can find him before I leave.

****

(Of course Nat did not know that September 11, the date he sailed for the Pacific, would become our wedding day 9 years later. Neither did I ... by now, I was 12 years old & Nat was nearly 19. We would not meet until May 20, 1952.)

(Camp Pendleton CA)
(Tue.) Sep. 11, 1945

Dear Folks,

Just time for a short note before I leave to board ship. Well, I guess this is it, the day we embark, and right now I can't tell whether I'm elated or dejected. I guess it's sort of a mixture of the two. I'll more than likely get a big kick out of a Pacific trip, but then of course I'm gonna miss the ol' U.S.A. At any rate, I should come back much wiser than when I went across. Also, there are a lot of guys over there who really deserve to be replaced, as they went through hell.

After while you should receive a card stating that I've arrived safely overseas. These are sent by the Navy Department when we reach our destination. It will give my address. However, after turning in the card, I was changed from D to E company. So when you receive the card just make that change. My overseas address should look like this:

Pvt. N.V. Wright Jr 996346 USMCR
Co. E, 81st Replacement Draft
% F.P.O.
San Francisco, California

Time to fall out so I better quit for now. I'm gonna try to get this mailed while on the way to the San Diego docks. While I'm gone I'll be thinking of you folks back home as you're the part of the U.S.A. I'll be coming home to some day.

Love to all, Bunk

* * * *

(This letter was dated in Hawaii 6 days after Nat's ship left San Diego & a day after it docked in Pearl Harbor.)

(Oahu, Hawaii)
(Mon.) September 17, 1945

Dear Folks,

After a five-day voyage, here I am in Hawaii. Our ship pulled into Pearl Harbor Sunday the 16th at about 1:00 P.M. The trip across was comparatively calm, except that we were pretty crowded (Uh-oh! Out of ink). We left San Diego Monday the 11th. The Red Cross filled us up with lemonade and doughnuts as we went up the gangplank. By about 6:00 P.M. we were out of sight of land. We had good weather all the way and the Pacific was the bluest water I've ever seen. There was always something doing aboard ship, even though it was crowded. There were movies on deck every night, and during the day there were boxing matches and a group of fellows formed a pretty good swing band. One big rub to being crowded was to be found in trips to the head. Space for the discharge of daily duties was very hard to find. Many a time aboard ship I wished that I had one of those "Gems of American Architecture" advertised in the book Mr. Carter gave me. Sal Marotti, one of my pals at Lejeune, worked in the ship's library and he got hold of a copy of "Life in a Putty Knife Factory" by H. Allen Smith for me. It's a sequel to "Low Man on a Totem Pole". It sure is a riot *(I read my brother's copies of these 2 books the same year because he said I was not allowed to read them while he was away in the Army!)*.

We slept in bunks stacked four deep like shelves. Just like sleeping in a closet. It was pretty cramped, but we spent most of our time on deck, so it wasn't so bad. Besides over 4,000 Marines, there were over 800 Sailors being transported to Pearl Harbor. So you can see I had plenty of company. We were on the USS General Weigel, a pretty big transport. It was an Army troop ship, manned by the Coast Guard and carrying Marines and Swabbies. Confoozin, ain't it?

As we neared the Hawaiian shore, the water changed gradually from blue to green. The whole Island of Oahu, where Pearl Harbor and Honolulu are, is covered, except for a flat coastal area, by a range of lofty, blue-green peaks that run right up into the clouds. The highest I've ever seen. Pearl Harbor was quiet and comparatively empty except for a couple of carriers and destroyers.

We boarded trucks at Pearl Harbor for the Marine Replacement Center where I am now quartered.

This place is about seven miles from Honolulu. It's made up mostly of "6-man" tents similar to the ones at Lejeune. There's also a nice outdoor theater, a football field, baseball diamond and a large PX & post office. We're right next to the highway that runs from Pearl Harbor to Honolulu, and there are cars, buses, trains, trucks, etc. passing by all the time. Honest! It's more civilized than Camp Lejeune!

They haven't straightened out our postal facilities yet, and they tell us we will not be able to mail any letters for a week until they do. So you'll probably receive my letters in a lump.

There goes chow-call. Gotta run. More later.

Love to all, Bunk

****

(Oahu, Hawaii)
(Wed.) Sept 19, 1945

Dear Mother,

I'm situated at the Marine Transient Center here in Hawaii, but for how long I don't know. The rumors are flying thick and fast as to where we'll go from here and when we'll leave. At any rate, I don't expect to be here more than a couple of weeks at the most. The most popular theory at present is that we will join the 2nd Division at Guam and go from there to Japan. Most all of our N.C.O.s have agreed that this is the most probable thing, and some N.C.O.s have even gone so far as to confirm it. However it's still unofficial as yet, and I've learned, from seven months in this most unpredictable of outfits, not to forecast the future or take anything for granted, and the unexpected usually happens. Our officers won't commit themselves on the subject of our future base, but they don't know for sure themselves. So as you can see, it's just one big guessing game.

Willie Hetrick was down here for a while but he had left by the time I got here. There are several fellows in my company who went through Field Music School at Parris Island with Willie before he was sent to Lejeune.

Our company is due for liberty soon so maybe I'll get to see Honolulu. I've seen little or none of this place so far. On one side of the camp is the highway to Honolulu and on the other side are those high, dark, blue-green mountains I was telling you about in my last letter. They sure are pretty. There are some WAVES barracks right in back of us, but there are also some very eagle-eyed M.P.s between us and them (Coises! Foiled again!). The buses that run by here look exactly like the Capital Transit buses. They are even painted like them. There are times when I'd swear that I saw an Anacostia or Hillcrest bus coming. That's a nostalgic touch.

Did you get my letter I wrote on the day we left for overseas? Hope everyone's fine at home. Well, I gotta quit 'cause there goes taps.

Love to all, Bunk

****

Dear Mother,

I'm situated for the present at the Marine Transient Center in Hawaii, but for how long I don't know. As I said in my last letter, the scuttlebutt is really stacking up, but as far as I know we should be here at least a couple more weeks.

This location here is a lot more modern and far better equipped than I expected. We even heard rumors on shipboard that we would have to sleep in pup tents just like on bivouac, so you can imagine the surprise we got when we came to a large, well-kept camp with ball fields, a large outdoor theater, a boxing arena, a big PX, etc. We're located next to the Pearl Harbor-Honolulu highway. It's a dual highway with a railroad track running down the middle between the lanes. So all day long we have planes, trains, trucks, cars, buses, Jeeps and sometimes even tanks going by. It's twice as civilized as Camp Lejeune. This place is considered the best Marine base in the Pacific. There are movies every night and stage shows once or twice a week. I've seen "Junior Miss" and "Incendiary Blonde" and numerous other movies and stage shows here. It's a plenty nice set-up.

Across the road from us is a big civilian housing area, where Navy civilian employees live. Also there's a baseball stadium where at present a Navy all-star series is being played with many former big league stars playing. I'm pretty certain of getting to see at least one game. Then I'll write *(cousin)* Bill and tell him all about it. I know he'd give anything to be able to see it.

My routine here consists of mostly organized athletics and some close-order drill. We get paid Tuesday and get liberty Wednesday. I'm going into Honolulu and do some shopping. 'Nuff for now.

Love to all, Bunk

* * * *

(Oahu, Hawaii)
(Thu.) Sept. 27, 1945

Dear Mother,

I finally got to see Honolulu. It was definitely more modern than I expected it to be, and there weren't as many palm trees as I expected to see. However there was plenty to do. There were amusement joints with shooting galleries, juke boxes, photo stands, etc. There were malted milk stands, curio & nick-nack shops, sidewalk restaurants, stands where you can buy pineapple juice and slices of pineapple, movies and three big U.S.O.s. The most popular concessions are the novelty photo studios where you can have your picture taken with a hula girl. (He did & I still have a copy.) Some are real Hawaiians while other girls are Chinese or just Stateside girls, but they all have grass skirts on anyway (o-o-O-O-O!).

Downtown Honolulu is built a lot like any American city, but the streets are narrower. However along the waterfront and in the outskirts, the architecture takes on a definite Oriental and Polynesian touch and the palm trees and shrubbery are more plentiful. Along the Northern edge of Honolulu runs that range of green, vegetated mountains I told you about. One unique thing I noticed were the houses perched precariously on the mountain sides. It reminded me of the cabins on the hillsides and mountains of northeastern Georgia.

I went shopping and bought some stuff to send home. I found an empty cardboard beer case to pack them in. Now mind you, this stuff is for Christmas, so when you receive the box, <u>don't</u> open it till Christmas or I'll tattle to Santa Claus.

Our mail-sending has been temporarily halted, as we have been alerted. We expect to leave for Guam soon. I'm still able to receive mail though. You'll probably receive several letters at once as I'll mail a bunch at the same time as soon as I am able.

I'm going to Waikiki next liberty.

'Nuff for now.

Love to all, Bunk

P.S. Let me know how long it takes this letter to go Free. *(Once away from the U.S. mainland, G.I.'s could still frank their mail, but it was delivered slowly by ship and/or overland. A 6c airmail stamp brought a G.I.'s mail home faster… hopefully!)*

****

(Oahu, Hawaii)
(Sun.) Sept. 30, '45

Dear Mother,

I went to Honolulu again today. I spent more time wandering around looking over the town. First I walked around the water front. This is where most of the Chinese live. There were a lot of seafood and chop suey joints, bars and markets. The streets were narrow, which helped add to the Oriental atmosphere. I also saw quite a few Chinese sitting in front of their shops making flower leis and chanting in sing-song fashion. Next I wandered around the outskirts near the foot of the mountain range. Sure was pretty.

The people here are generally short, except for some of the pure Hawaiians. They dress and act like Americans. They seem to like swing almost as much as their native hula tunes. Also, they are nuts about football. It's not uncommon to see barefoot kids kicking a football around. They have a well organized inter-high football league established here.

I saw "Weekend at the Waldorf" and "The Story of G.I. Joe" this week. They sure were swell. The stage play "Kiss and Tell" will be given here soon. I've heard that it's a riot. We sure get the tops in entertainment around here. However, before long we'll be pretty far away from it, so I better enjoy it while I can.

Say, by the way, I'm drinking coffee now. The milk we get here is that powdered stuff which tastes more like Milk of Magnesia. There is no fresh milk, so I developed a taste for coffee. Don't worry, that's the only extra habit I have acquired. For the most part, I'm just the same obnoxious me.

I mailed that box of stuff home yesterday. Remember, that's Christmas stuff, so don't open it till then. Let me know when you receive the box.

The only thing I really want for Christmas are snapshots of the family. The ones I have now are kinda faded from bivouac at Camp Lejeune.

Love to all, Bunk

****

(This was penned to sister Pat on the occasion of her 17th birthday.)

(Oahu, Hawaii)
(Thu.) Oct. 4, '45

Dear Pat,

Well, I guess you feel pretty big today ~ being all of 17. Practically middle-aged. Sure wish I could be there to deliver the swats in person. Oh well, I guess between the runt and Pop, your "pride" is pretty sore (H-m-m-m! wearing it a little low this season, eh?). I feel bad about not being able to send you something, but after mailing that beer case full of Christmas stuff home, I found myself slightly flat. Maybe I'll be home next "nock-over-four". *(That is what Pat called her birth date, October 4, when she was a small child.)*

I went to Waikiki yesterday. Gosh, what a beautiful place. There's a wide, white, sandy beach, and palm trees galore. The ocean is a pretty blue-green. I saw quite a few native boys skimming on the crest of the waves (not the gals, the ocean) on surfboards and outriggers. Along the highway near the beach are movies, bowling alleys, photo stands, a miniature golf course and counters selling pineapple slices and ice cold milk shakes (Slurp! slurp!). I also saw quite a few well-stacked babes (Hubba-hubba-hubba!). At the east end of Waikiki is a high, rocky peak. I walked around the base of it but didn't have time to climb it *(This was Diamond Head. At his insistence, Nat & I made this climb in 1989. He was exhilarated. I was near death!)*. In the box I sent home there are presents for everyone but Pop. I couldn't find anything that he would like. Please get something for him for Christmas and I'll send you the dough when I get it.

Well, I gotta run now. More later.

Love, Nat

P.S. Thanks for keeping me posted on the school team.
P.P.S. Again, happy birthday.
****

(Guam)
(Mon.) Oct. 29, '45

Dear Mother,

I am now on Guam. We got in last night after a nine-day ride from Pearl Harbor on an aircraft carrier. I sure got a big kick out of the trip. I wish I could adequately describe it. We left Oct. 18 and boarded the carrier, U.S.S. Cardi. It was a carrier of the smaller class used in the Atlantic Patrol during the war. It had about 25 subs to its credit. After the war, it was sent to the Pacific to be used as a transport. We were assigned bunks in the hold below the hangar, but I took my bedroll up and slept on the flight deck, where it was cooler. There were 12 planes on the flight deck.

Down in the hangar were basketball and volleyball courts, and we were shown movies every night. *(Nat has told me that when a movie was shown on board a troop ship, the screen was in the middle of the hold & the guys sat on both sides, so to accommodate more bodies. Because Nat could read backwards writing, he sat on the "wrong" side & was assigned to read letters or any written word to his shipmates on that side.)*

The chow was pretty good and we had turkey on Navy Day. The weather was swell except for a few thunder showers when we were three days from Guam. During the day, I spent most of my time sitting squarely astride the bow. That salt breeze sure felt good and the ocean is unbelievably blue, almost indigo. Our carrier had gunnery practice a couple of times. I sure got a belt out of watching the Navy gun crews in action. We had rifle inspections every day on the flight deck, but they weren't too strict about them. I did considerable reading during the trip. I read a couple of novels, one of which, "Men against the Sea", a sequel to "Mutiny on the Bounty", I enjoyed especially well as I read it sitting in my favorite position on the bow, and the rolling Pacific provided background.

We pulled into Guam Harbor about 1:00 P.M. after passing the nearby Isle of Rota. In the harbor were Naval craft of near every kind, including a huge carrier of the Hornet class. There was also a captured Jap ship anchored there, manned by Jap prisoners.

Before we left Pearl Harbor our mail-sending was held up several times. I left letters I wrote on the 9th, 14th, & 18th of October with a fellow to mail. I hope you got them. *(Those letters are not among the saved ones. My bet is that "a fellow" did not mail them.)*

Everyone is totally broke, but we get paid in a day or two. I'm waiting till I can buy some air mail stamps before I mail this, as it'll travel quicker.

There goes taps. More later.

Love to all, Bunk

Please excuse the pencil ~ no pen, no ink!!

* * * *

Dear Mother,

I'm now located at the Transient Center here on Guam, but for how long I don't know. I've been moved five times to different tents since arriving. I hope they don't move me before I finish this letter.

I guess you'd like to know something about this rock. Well, Here goes. Guam is the southern-most island of the Marianas. It's about 26 miles long and about seven miles wide. The place is very thickly vege-tated, mostly by coconut palms, breadfruit trees and other tropical trees. It rains every day, but not for very long, and there's plenty of sunshine and it gets plenty hot! The place we live in is a big clearing hacked right out of the jungle. We live in the regulation 16x16-foot six-man tents, but they're in pretty sad shape. They're always springing leaks and tears. There are little toads that hop all over the place here. A couple of times I have awakened to find some of the little beggars hopping all over the foot of my sack (Oh well, it beats pink elephants anyway!).

The chow here is pretty much stinkeroo and the coffee tastes like embalming fluid. However, we are expected to shove off for the Orient (more than likely Japan) any day now, so we won't have to cope with it very long. At least the chow can't be any worse in Japan! The liberty around here isn't so hot. You can't go to native villages and you can't go into the jungle. The only places left are other military bases. We have a PX and an outdoor theater on this base, so everybody is pretty con-tent to stay here.

I've had quite a few coconuts. They were plenty good but I wish you were here to bake 'em in a cake. Fellows who have been here quite a while say that this joint gets pretty monotonous. In fact, they say it eventually causes some guys to act sort of odd. There are rumors of fel-lows swinging through the trees nude and beating their chests. However this is rather far-fetched. Nevertheless, I have seen some guys wearing earrings and some with big handlebar mustaches. I saw one fellow with a little red pom-pom hanging on each waxed handlebar of his mustache. Odd, eh what?

There are quite a few Jap prisoners here on Guam. There are also a few uncaptured Japs running loose in the hills and jungles. These are more or less living like animals. They seldom ever molest military bases. They mostly prowl around native villages. Little or no disturbances are caused by them except for a few instances when one attacks a native. However, the other night, a marine truck driver was shot by a prowling

Jap. Subsequently, our company was given guard duty over a sector along a small road at the edge of the jungle. You sure hear funny noises in the jungle at night. The birds screech and chatter and the wind causes the palm leaves to rustle, making a sort of rattling sound like someone running a stick along a picket fence. There are many other unexplainable sounds. I also saw quite a few large bats flying among the trees. Boy! What material for "The Inner Sanctum" radio show.

Our mail caught up to us today. I sure was glad to find a couple letters for me. I got a letter from Willie Hetrick right before I shipped out of Hawaii. He is in the 23rd Regiment Band on the island of Maui in Hawaii. I'm glad he got back into the band.

We have been issued winter clothes. We got high-top shoes, thick wool sox, long underwear, wool shirts, a fur-lined jacket, wind proof pants, caps with earflaps, mittens, a muffler and a big wool sleeping bag. I sure wish I could get hold of some of that winter gear for Pop to use during ducking season, but the quartermaster is pretty stingy. I'm pretty sure we are heading soon for Japan. 108 men out of E Co. left yesterday, more than likely for Japan. I was left here with a small group of E Co. fellows who will ship out with the rest of the 81st.

I managed to borrow an air mail stamp to mail a letter I wrote on Oct. 29th. As soon as I finish this, I'm gonna see if I can't bum one to mail this one. We are due to get paid in a day or so. Then I'm gonna buy a stack of air mail stamps. Mail takes too long to go free.

Let me know when that box of stuff I mailed from Hawaii gets home. I had it insured, so it should make it O.K. I wish I could have sent Pat something for her birthday, but I was financially minus at the time. I hope I can make up for it next time.

Hey! What do ya' know?! Today I'm a veteran of 8 months in this outfit. Tempus sure fugits, doesn't it? *(So now we know he arrived at Parris Island on March 1, 1945).*

I hope everyone is fine at home. I'll bet the Runt is really starting to sprout up. And maybe even that good looking 17-year-old sister of mine is beginning to grow a little, too. Who knows? Weirder things have happened.

Time for chow (and I use the word "chow" loosely).

Love to all, Bunk

****

(When Nat did not have enough news to engage sister Pat's attention [& sometimes when he did], he composed for her some "Tall Tales". This letter is a prime example, a double-header.)

(Guam)
(Mon.) Nov. 5, '45

Dear Pat,

Long time no hear. I imagine that's what you're saying as you read this. One of my far too few letters to you. I wonder if the day will ever come when I will be in one spot long enough to get my correspondence going with some degree of consistency. I was moved five times in Hawaii, and I've been here only about a week, yet I've been moved to different quarters four times already. I'll soon be placed in a division and in a regular outfit, so I should get comparatively settled then, I hope. We are expected to shove off for the Orient, more than likely Japan, soon. We've been issued winter clothing here, even long underwear (with no reet seat with a flap trap, durn it!). There is a possibility that they may send us to China, what with the trouble kicking up there. However, Japan is more probable, so the majority of our officers & N.C.O.s think.

Gosh, sometimes I can hardly believe it's me making this trip. For a guy who was never farther west before than Glen Echo, I'm really getting around. I wish I could adequately describe the kick I'm getting out of this trip. I guess before it's over, I should be able to write a small geography book. Hawaii was really a wonderful place. I thoroughly enjoyed every liberty pass I had there. I also got a big belt out of the voyages on the ocean, especially the carrier trip from Pearl Harbor to Guam. I got my first real look at the jungle here on Guam. I also saw a couple of native villages and several bombed-out missions, earmarks of war.

All in all, this has proved a very interesting place. However, our location here isn't so hot. Our tents are in pretty sad shape, always springing leaks and rips, and the chow is pretty much el stinko. The Army and Navy (commonly referred to as "doggies" and "swabjockos") live in steel Quonset huts. Oh well, the Marine Corps usually gets what's left over in the way of facilities, so we're used to it. And besides, the fellows who were here a year or so ago had nothing but the mud to live in so I've no cause to beef. No matter where you go, there's always some bellyaching, which is no more than healthy.

Referring back to the chow, which is a widely discussed subject hereabouts, several of my buddies have been seen lately with broken jaws. It seems they stuck their forks in the meat and it whinnied and kicked back. To further substantiate my story, I pointed to the tortured morsel of meat on my tray and said to the mess sergeant nearby, "How far did you have to chase this horse before he gave up from exhaustion?" And without batting an eye lash, he responded, "Nine miles". Ya just can't win. And in regard to the coffee, the stuff they serve us seems to have the caliber of high-octane stove polish. The other morning my buddy, Hal Wood from Birmingham, Alabama, took a hefty snort of his java and his eyes subsequently lit up like a pin ball machine and from his ears a little sign emerged reading "tilt". Not wishing to suffer Woodie's fate, I tossed mine out the window. It seems it landed on a palm tree. As a result, the tree trembled, wilted, and the coconuts shriveled to the size of moth balls. When I related the incident to that genial gent, the mess sergeant, he indignantly replied, "What the hell did you expect, chimes?" Woe is us!

And now comes an ever popular topic, the head (Other synonyms: willie, biffie, Johnny, Jake, dooley, etc., courtesy of "Gems of American Architecture"). An excursion to this sanctum of evacuation is quite a venture. Allow me to relate to you in satirical form a typical pilgrimage to such an abode. First you dictate your will and make a last-minute check on your insurance papers. Then, (after a final tactical briefing in the ready room), you don your trusty gas mask, pick up your 40-millimeter anti-aircraft gun and take off for the "cone" house. As you charge across no-man's land, you observe that your approach is barred by several echelons of mosquitoes escorted by B-29s. However, you are spared because, as the mosquitoes swoop low, they look at your dog tags and discover that your blood is not their type.

You somehow manage to reach the "half-moon" house with at least one limb intact and, stepping inside, you notice that it is a well-constructed commode, an eight-holer on a ten-hole chassis, strongly supported in the foundation by the bodies of poor unfortunate souls who lacked the stamina to undergo the ordeal. You heave a sigh of relief as you have made it. You are of the elite few who have achieved the goal. But then as you begin to disrobe for the ceremony, you glance down at the toilet seat. And horror of horrors! What do you see but square holes instead of the conventional round ones?! The shock proves too great and you slump to the turf in a swoon and are carted off, muttering insensibly, to your upholstered cell in the psycho ward. Ah me! Such is life! Brutal, ain't it?

From your letters and clippings I'd say the school team is doing swell. There are two fellows from *(rival D.C. high school)* Tech in my company and I'm making it pretty hard for them to forget that 9-0 game in which our Injuns racked 'em up in the side pocket. Thanks for keeping me posted on the games.

How's the sorority doing? Be sure and send me that picture you promised me of the "She-Wolf-Society" in their sweaters (Hubba-hubba-hubba). I foolishly told these eager beavers in my tent that you would send me such a picture and now they drool down my collar every time I get a letter.

It's almost time for chow so I better knock off for now.

Give my love to all at home.

Love, Nat

****

Dear Mother,

It happened again. Yep, I was moved again. I have been placed in Co. D of the 81st. There were only 35 of us left in E Co., so they moved us to D Co. I haven't the slightest idea why I wasn't sent out with the rest of E Co. As I said in my last letter, 108 men out of E Co. were shipped out to Japan. 35 of us weren't needed, so we stayed behind. They just picked the names at random. We have been told that the rest of the 81st will ship out any day now, but still we sit. We are more or less marking time till we leave. We are doing guard duty, mess duty and working details.

I'm glad to say that I've been able to devote more time to church. The services have been swell, and I know I've gotten a lot out of them. I guess it took the Marine Corps to make me realize the importance of the church. I hope I don't neglect it when I get back to civilian life. The chaplain I had at Parris Island shipped out, where to I don't know. So I don't know how I can straighten out the matter of my confirmation and enrollment in St. Timothy's with Rev. Coleman. You said in one of your letters that he had not received any word from P.I. of my confirmation and church enrollment. Maybe if you sent me his address, I could write to Rev. Coleman and explain it to him. I sure would like to get it straightened out. (*Nat was an active Episcopalian all his adult life. I, a lifelong Lutheran, was told I must "convert" in order be married in the Episcopal Church. He & I shared a love for the Church & were lay ministers for many years.*)

How's the weather over thar' now? I guess the air is getting quite a nip to it. The other day I was listening to the radio belonging to one of our sergeants and I heard a recorded re-broadcast of the Redskins-Giants football game of a couple weeks ago in which the skins won 24-15 (I think that was the score). It sure sounded funny to hear the announcer say, "There's an invigorating nip in the air of this frosty October afternoon", when it's hot enough here to make everyone feel lazy all the time (and as you well know, being lazy comes natural for me). Speaking of football, judging from the clippings & stuff Pat has sent me, Anacostia seems to be making them sit up and take notice. Remember how much fun Pop used to have in ribbing me about the school team? Well, this year our "Injuns" have done pretty good, but I'll bet that Central game gave him plenty of material to razz Pat about.

Oh, by the way, I received the first issue of the Pow-Wow *(high school paper)* today. I sure was glad to get it. Even though I did set some sort of record as a dead end kid there, I still like to keep tabs on the ol' brain factory. Some of the most fun I ever had in my life was had in school. And I guess, by some weird means or another, I did learn something. I fully intend to take advantage of the G.I. Bill of Rights educational program. I'd like to go to Washington College in Chestertown and take up a literary course as sort of a background before I delve into art. Of course I could take art right along with it so as not to lose touch with it. At any rate, I would like to take a literary course because, as Miss Dickey once told me, art and literature are closely connected and besides, some day I intend to try a little writing on the side. At any rate, it wouldn't hurt to be a little broad-minded. As soon as I get settled in a regular outfit, I'm going to see about taking a refresher course in English grammar and literature from the Marine Corps Institute. A lot of fellows are taking correspondence courses from the Institute and they say it's very helpful. I'm going to look into it.

How's everyone feeling at home? Swell, I hope. As for me, I feel fine. I still weigh a bit over 140 and have suffered no ills except a little touch of ringworm, which has now dried up. The chow has improved and, for the past few days, we've been getting sugar for our coffee. For a couple of weeks, there wasn't a grain on the island. To everyone's surprise and delight, we had a chicken dinner on November 10, the 170th birthday of the Corps. There was also free beer for all but I didn't want any (I can't grow on that stuff).

Now look, Mammy, I don't want you to start worrying about that incident about that uncaptured Jap wounding a Marine guard that I mentioned in one of my previous letters from here. That was only the second incident of that kind that has occurred on this post since it was built well over a year ago. There are, as I said before, only a small number of Japs wandering around the jungle and they bother mostly native villagers once in a great while and seldom ever come near a military reservation. A couple of 'em straggled in last week and gave themselves up. They were so miserably skinny and so scared they could hardly walk. The Japs that are prisoners of war here have no desire to escape. In fact they are very meek and follow their guards around like sheep. They're slick little beggars. They know they can live and eat better as prisoners than prowling around by themselves. So you've no cause to worry.

Several packages have come from home. Thanks ever so much. I really do appreciate them. They are one part of the U.S.A. I can carry with me. I don't want you to go to a lot of trouble for me but I sure would like some snapshots of the family. Some of the ones I have now were faded while on bivouac at Camp Lejeune.

I was glad to hear that the box I sent from Hawaii arrived O.K. I hope you succeed in keeping Pat (Alias Mr. Keene, tracer of hidden Christmas packages) out of it till Dec. 25th. Almost chow time so I better knock off for now. Hug the Runt for me.

Love to all, Bunk

****

(Guam)
(Tue.) Nov. 20, '45

Dear Mother,

Today we were alerted and given the information as to when we leave. The entire 81st Draft will board an Army transport Thursday, Nov. 22 (Thanksgiving Day) and will be carried to the 2nd Marine Division, which, as far as we know, is in Japan. I'm glad that I'm finally going to join a regular outfit as maybe now I'll get somewhat settled and things should be better organized. I've heard a lot of stories about duty in Japan (if that's where we're going, and I'm pretty sure it is), but I'll only know when I get there ("natch"). Just the idea of going to the Orient is intriguing. In fact, I find it kinda' hard to believe. I can remember looking over at a map of the Orient in school and wondering if someday I might get to see it. Well, it looks like I will after all and I guess I'll have something to tell tall tales to my grandkids about.

Oops! There goes chow call. I'll continue this when I get back.

Cheese n' crackers! Another change. Our orders have been changed and we leave tomorrow, the 21st, instead of Thursday the 22nd. Honest, the way they run this outfit reminds me of the Washington government bureaus. You can't predict nothing nohow. Well, I better cut this short as I have some fast and furious packing to do tonight. I'll write as soon as I get where we're going, which should be in 3 or 4 days at the most.

Love to all, Bunk

P.S. Happy Thanksgiving

****

Nagasaki, Japan
(Thu.) Nov. 29, 1945

Dear Mother,

I finally dood it. I've set foot on Japanese soil. On Nov. 27th we landed at Nagasaki on Kyushu, the southern-most Jap home island. After a 5-day trip from Guam, we put into Sasebo, a port about 200 miles from Nagasaki, on the 25th. However, due to some mix-up in the orders, this proved to be the wrong port. So we stayed there until the morning of the 27th when we sailed for Nagasaki. We went ashore in landing craft. Nagasaki is mainly situated in a valley surrounded by mountains and high terraced hills.

However, we landed in an outlying waterfront district located on the sides and at the base of several very steep hills. The terrain of this country is like nothing I've ever seen before. It goes shooting up sharply into the steep hills and mountains. One thing uniquely characteristic of the countryside is the intricate terracing of the hillsides into farmland. At a distance, these hillsides look like a flight of multi-colored steps. The living quarters of the poorer class Japanese consist mostly of squatty, flimsily-paneled houses with wide windows and low, gently-curving, tile roofs. Many of the houses have no windows or flooring and nearly all are dirty.

We were met on the docks by scores of dirty-faced Jap kids of various sizes and ages. The boys were wearing high-buttoned military jackets, the older boys wearing long pants somewhat like riding pants, and the younger boys wearing shorts. The girls wore kimonos of many colors and wooden sandals. Some of the boys wore sandals, while others wore boots and odd-looking shoes with a finger-like projection for the big toe. While waiting for trucks we talked to them, making ourselves understood by sign language. A couple fellows had Jap-English dictionaries. *(Nat had one eventually & he about wore it out. It moved with us wherever we lived.)* I asked one 8-year-old Jap schoolboy to write his name on a piece of paper. I am enclosing the piece of paper plus a Jap coin that I traded him a nickel for. *(Both paper & coin are long gone.)* It sure was an interesting experience. I ought to have a lot to tell you after my first liberty pass.

We are quartered in a former prisoner-of-war camp located in a pretty little valley about three miles from Nagasaki. The barracks consist of flimsy two-storied buildings with tile roofs. There are no heating facilities at present and at night it gets plenty cold. However, they have promised us stoves.

The mail situation is plenty fouled up and probably will remain so until I get put into a regular outfit. I've been told that we won't be able to mail any letters for a few days, but I'll mail this as soon as possible. Don't worry about me. I feel fine.

Uh-oh! Chow time. More later.

Love to all, Bunk

****

Nagasaki, Japan
(Fri.) Dec. 14, 1945

Dear Mother,

A lot has happened since I last wrote. I am writing this on borrowed stationery with a borrowed pen. Also I am wearing borrowed underwear and a borrowed coat. In my pocket I have 20 yen and 80 sen (which amounts to about a dollar and 38 cents in American money). In fact, I'm about as rich as one of the "Okies" in "The Grapes of Wrath".

All this is the result of a fire which yesterday burned five barracks and a recreation center to the ground and put 700 men out of a home. Now for gawsh sake, don't start worrying. I am perfectly O.K. Only three men were seriously hurt and they are being taken care of now at the division hospital. I was in the mess hall serving chow when the fire started about 6 A.M. in the barracks of Headquarters Company, about a half a mile away. Nearly everyone left the hall at once, but, as there were still a few fellows in the chow line, I had to stay and serve chow. By the time I was able to get away, all the barracks had caved in except A Company's, which was on the end of the row and was just bursting into flames. I knew then that my gear was lost because our barracks was right next to Headquarters barracks and was the second building to go.

I then found three of my buddies who were also on mess duty and were quartered in the same room as I was. However, that morning they didn't have to report early to the mess hall, so they stayed in their sacks. They told of waking up and looking out the window, seeing Headquarters barracks on fire, with flames shooting across the narrow 15-yard courtyard between the two buildings. Within a few minutes, our room was filled with smoke and the outer walls had caught fire. The fellows had just time enough to get themselves and a few scant pieces of equipment out before our barracks was a raging inferno. No sooner had they gotten out when three bazooka shells that some damn fool had stolen and hidden in his seabag exploded in the room next to ours. Luckily the blast hurt no one, but it sure made a loud bang and helped to bring the barracks down quicker.

It was amazing to see the rapidity with which the blaze swept through the rows of barracks. They were built of light, dry, flimsy wood which burned like tinderboxes. Inside of ten minutes, Headquarters barracks was flat and our barracks was almost gone. By the time I arrived from the mess hall, everything was leveled except A Co.'s barracks and the recreation hall. There were fellows running here and there carrying equipment they had managed to save. Some had packs, while others had seabags or bedding rolls and a few had rifles. The fellows in A and B Co. had time to save quite a bit of gear. However, Headquarters Co. and C Co. were unable to save an awful lot of stuff.

I helped some fellows in A Co. carry some gear clear of the barracks. We had to work fast though as the building was smoke-filled and the heat was terrific. It wasn't long before flames went licking up the walls and the building burst into flames with a roar. We managed, most of us, to get clear of the barracks in time. However, three fellows were trapped upstairs. One of them made a running feet-first dive down the stairs and made it out the door. The other two came out the second story window. One guy knocked the window panes out by hurling a seabag thru it. He then followed the seabag with a jump to the ground below. The other fellow was more cautious and hung dangling from the window sill, trying to claw out a foothold in the wall. However, the windowsill itself caught on fire and he was forced to let go. None of the three was hurt seriously. The fellow who jumped from the window, however, landed very unceremoniously in a drainage ditch and hurt his - uh - pride.

The rec hall went down shortly afterward and that was that. All this, five two-story barracks and a rec hall burned flat as a griddle cake in less than 45 minutes. We saved some empty barracks across the street by throwing water on 'em and hacking away parts that had caught fire from burning sparks. There were two fire engines there from Nagasaki, but they were pretty antiquated and had leaky hoses that gave off about as much of a stream of water as a fox terrier in a hedge row. The Jap villagers from the nearby town of Tomachi arrived on the scene with a crude fire-fighting apparatus pulled by a very sleepy horse. It worked by means of a hand pump and gave off about a pint of water per hour. So you can see we were pretty poorly equipped and the fire ran generally unchecked.

At the time of the fire's start, A Co. was in the mess hall eating, B Co. was marching to the mess hall, C Co. had just fallen out of their barracks for chow, and Headquarters Co. was still inside. There were a few fellows from Headquarters Co. who were just barely able to make it outside in their scivvy drawers. The fellows who were in my room when the fire started were unable to get any of my equipment out, as it was over next to the window and was the first stuff in the room to start burning.

At the end of the fire, I took account of my losses. My sea bag, bedding roll, pack, rifle, helmet, toilet articles and all my personal gear were destroyed. At present I possess one pair of dungaree pants, one dungaree jacket, one flannel shirt, one pair of shoes and socks, my mess gear, one candy bar, a can of salted peanuts and my wallet. I was carrying or wearing these articles at the time.

Don't worry. We get a new clothing issue tomorrow and will get paid very soon, so I'll make out O.K. We have been moved to new barracks about a mile away. We will be here only a couple days and then we'll be sent to a regular outfit somewhere here on Kyushu.

Among the things burned in the fire were several letters I had written and had ready to mail as soon as they got our postal facilities straightened out. There was a birthday card I had made for Pop on the 2nd of December, and two other letters I had written on the 7th and 10th of December. Postal facilities have straightened out somewhat and I did manage to mail one letter and a Second Marine Division Christmas card home. *(I still have the card.)* My mail should go out more regularly now. I hope so.

I am now in C Co. of the 81st. I was put in C Co. when D Co. left last week to join a Signal battalion at Sasebo, 200 miles from here. They only needed a certain quota, so some had to be left behind. They left the last six men on the company roster behind and I was next to last, so I was selected, along with five others. We were put on mess duty and have been on mess duty ever since. That's two companies that have shipped out and left me behind (I must have B.O.).

I've gotta get back to the mess hall so I better knock off for now.

Have a Merry Christmas and please don't worry about me.

Love to all, Bunk

(Nat never mentions in later letters how the burned items were replaced. He had a beat-up, holey <u>Army</u> blanket among his possessions when we married, & he told me that they had gotten some low-quality replacements from a "Doggie" [Army] outfit after the fire. That was our car emergency blanket for years. I think some emergency occurred which lost the blanket to us forever.)

****

Nagasaki, Japan
(Sun.) Dec. 16, 1945

Dear Pat,

Here I am. I remember sitting in school looking at a map of this place and wondering if maybe someday I'd get to see it, but I never expected to. Uh-oh, we're falling out for some reason. More later.

Later -

We just got the word that we are leaving tomorrow. Our draft has been split up into groups to be sent to various regiments and battalions all over Kyushu. I am to join the 2nd Regiment about 200 miles from here (I think). I got your birthday card and picture. It really was swell.

Well, I gotta rush now as I have to get ready. It's snowing to beat the band and it's plenty chilly (understatement). I'll write you a long one very soon as I'll have plenty to write about.

So long for now.

Love, Nat

P.S. Discontinue using my draft address. I'll send you my new one as soon as possible.

****

Miyakonojo, Japan
(Thu.) Dec 20, 1945

Dear Pat,

Honest, I'm beginning to think that all I'll be good for when I get out of this outfit is a hobo. From the way I've moved around, one would think I had B.O. (No cracks, please. I'll have you know I make it a point to take a shower at least once a year whether I need it or not). At any rate, I am now in K Co., 3rd Battalion, 2nd Regiment, 2nd Marine Division . At last I am situated in what is known as a regular outfit and maybe now the mail will finally get straightened out. To give you an idea of how fouled up it has been, on December 12th, the day before the fire, I received a chain letter from the frat that was mailed on August 18th. However, that same day I received a letter from you dated about the first of December. You figure it out. I give up.

We are located about a mile and a half from Miyakonojo (pronounced Mee-yah-kon-o-jo) in north central Kyushu *(It's in the south - this was Nat's error - it is corrected in a later letter.)*, about 250 miles from Nagasaki. It's a pretty good-sized town, or at least it was. It was bombed a few times and right much damage was done. The town and camp are located on a wide, level plain surrounded by blue-gray mountains. We traveled here by train from Nagasaki in day coaches that were more like street cars. Believe me, it was a pretty cold trip. It's a good thing that there weren't any brass monkeys along on that trip or - uh - well, you know what would have happened (or have you ever heard that gag?).

Our barracks are a lot better than the ones in Nagasaki. We are living in former Japanese garrison barracks. They are made of heavier wood and, under American supervision, have been weather-proofed to some extent. When the draft broke up, most of my buddies were spread all over the island. However, two of my buddies who were with me at Pearl Harbor and Guam are in my company now. They are (stand by for a mouthful) Al Zieglmeier of Minnesota and Pete Wojculewicz of Connecticut. We, Zieglmeier, Wojculewicz, and Van Wert Wright IV, are the "unpronounceable three" of K Co.

Hal Wood, of Birmingham, Alabama, was sent to a Signal battalion at Sasebo. I'm sure gonna' miss him. We had barrels of fun at Pearl Harbor and Guam. Oh, by the way, here's a little bit of data about Woodie that you can relay to Ann Ferguson. I remember your telling me that she is from Birmingham. Here goes. He is 18, about 5 feet 10, blonde, and has a smile as broad as a cotton field. He's got plenty of personality plus. He likes to talk about his capabilities as a Casanova, but it affords good listening, so nobody minds. Really a great guy. He was born in Tuscaloosa and moved to Birmingham about 5 years ago. He went to Phillips High. He used to live in South Birmingham, I think it was around 35th Street, but recently moved to the Northside, around 17th Street. That's a pretty general picture, but it should help. If further information is required, please refer to Encyclopedia Britannica, section XVII, clause 6-7/8, entitled Genus Gyrenus, or poor wandering Marines. Next question please, Mr. Fadiman (Oops! Wrong program!).

While stationed at Nagasaki, I went out on liberty a couple of times. I sure got an immense kick out of what I saw. "Zig" and "Woj" (These are the nicknames we gave Zieglmeier & Wojculewicz so as to simplify pronunciation) and Woody and I all started out together. Just as we got out of the camp entrance, a lieutenant picked us up in a jeep, and, after tediously cramming ourselves in (at which I was an old hand, being a veteran of those Anacostia bus rides), we tore away and began zooting around the ridges and over the hilltops of the tortuous road that led from our camp to town. The fellows were all disposed to drop a sizeable stack of clinkers but I consoled them by telling them about those jet-propelled jaunts that Pop used to take us on whenever we shoved off for the Eastern Shore.

We got out at Tomachi. That's the little waterfront section of Nagasaki where our landing craft beached. This section is character-ized by an almost strangulating fish odor, very narrow alleys, squatty, rickety houses and battered fishing smacks and junks tied to ramshackle docks.

We proceeded from there to the main section of Nagasaki. There were men in discarded military garb (these were demobilized soldiers) moving about sullenly. There were women in multi-colored kimonos carrying babies on their backs papoose style, and young girls in slacks pigeon-toeing by (They looked more like chimpanzees than girls). The Japs, as a whole, are cold and sullen toward Americans except of course the beggars and the shopkeepers, who are out for your dough.

This, however, isn't true of the small kids, the ones who haven't gotten large enough to be sly and sneaky. They're a riot. Little shaven-headed boys in short pants and little girls with bowl-like hair cuts came tagging along behind us chattering and laughing. They are accom-plished mimics. They repeat anything they hear (that they can pro-nounce, of course). Some greeted us with cries of "Hullo" and one little wise guy about 7 years old managed to stammer out, "Greetings, Gate".

The most popular exclamation is "Hubba! Hubba!" which they chorus forth gleefully at every opportunity.

Woodie and Woj attempted to teach three of the little gremlins "You Are My Sunshine". We were amazed to find that they could, in a somewhat broken manner, master the first couple lines. We gave them some gum and a couple of oranges and continued on our way. They left us, yelling, "Goo-bye". The streets in downtown Nagasaki are somewhat wider than its suburbs, but motor traffic is very much a hazard to pedestrians. There were quite a few wrecked and half-torn-down buildings. However, this was not the section of town that the atom bomb hit. We saw many small, narrow shops and markets. There were also quite a few dingy little restaurants, which were out of bounds to us because of the high disease rate. We watched the Nips eating with chop sticks. I'd starve to death before I could get any nourishment eating that way. The other day I tried using a pair in the mess hall, and before I had gotten two mouthfuls in I nearly poked 3 teeth out and stuck the damn things up my nostrils.

We continued on past a couple of Jap movie theaters and wandered into a couple of large department stores which, besides Japanese household articles, displayed kimonos, fans, dolls, table cloths, purses, tea sets and many other miscellaneous items. The most interesting shop, however, was a small art store in which they had many examples of Japanese art. The scenes depicted mostly mountains, farms, pagodas and fishing boats. I found one watercolor of a domestic scene showing a woman fondly thumping her beloved spouse on the head with a parasol. Touching, what? I bought a whole armload to send home but they burned up, along with some fans, purses and some other articles I had bought, in that fire we had a week or so ago.

In the same shop there was a caricature artist who for 20 yen (about $1.38), painted carricatures on white silk handkerchiefs. I had mine painted (It looked more like Mussolini than me. Oh well, flattery won't get him anywhere). This, too, burned up (It probably started the fire).

In the streets of Nagasaki were many little piles of rubble and almost all the windows were broken and boarded up. From there we boarded another antiquated-looking street car bound for the north side of the city where the atom bomb hit *(on August 9, 1945)*. This is where we saw the real damage.

We got out of the car at the railroad station. Past this point is where the bomb radius begins. When I first saw the leveled and wrecked buildings, it reminded me of our house after a frat party. Seriously though, I have never seen such utter destruction. It was like a vast, endless desert of ruin. Everything was reduced to crumbled bits of brick and framework, with the exception of a few leaning steel frames of factories and an occasional dead hulk of a tree or the tottering remains of a wall or an archway which jutted out sharply against a drab gray sky. A drear mist seems to hang about the place at all times, sort of like a ghostly afterthought.

We walked through a tangled maze of smashed machinery and brick rubble. This was all that was left of the large Mitsubishi aircraft factories in this area. Past this, on a hill top, were the almost unrecognizable ruins of the homes of the factory workers. Among the wreckage, we could see bits of clothing, pottery and other household articles. There were droves of people moving about probing around in the rubble, salvaging anything they could. This has been going on ever since about a week or so after the bomb hit. One interesting thing we noticed was that the women carried the heaviest loads (A bully idea). Some men had horses, but they must have been bachelors or else they would have had their wives working.

Almost time for taps, so I better quit for now. Please send me *(Cousins)* Dinny's and Sud's addresses. I'm ashamed of myself for losing contact with them. And tell Penny Murphy I'm answering her letter as soon as I finish this. I received her letter the day after I got to Nagasaki. More later.

Love to all, Nat

****

Miyakonojo, Japan
(Mon.) Dec. 24, 1945

Dear Mother,

Christmastime is here again and even though it is far from the merriest one I've ever had, it has been about as pleasant as possible under the circumstances. I have just come back from Christmas Eve services at the regimental chapel. It was about the best service I've attended since I've been in the Corps. The chapel was decorated beautifully with wreaths on the door and windows and a Christmas tree in one corner. On the tree were strips of red cellophane, painted pine cones, and a string of braided red cord serving as tinsel. There were dabs of cotton on the ends of the branches, simple but very attractive. We sang quite a few carols and the chaplain told the famous old Christmas story from the bible. It was really a swell service. At church I met a couple of my buddies who left Guam before I did and are now stationed a few miles from here.

Even though everyone is far from home tonight, we're making the best of it and everybody is in pretty good spirits, especially the boys over at the slop chute who are full of spirits up to the ears. All the beer is free tonight and believe me the "yoint is yumpin". I haven't had any beer (I still don't like the stuff), but they are also giving out free Cokes and I've guzzled enough so as to enable me to emit a few very masterful belches (Some of them comparable even to the voluminous belches belched by Cousin Willy and Uncle Ralph).

We were given little Red Cross boxes today containing candy, gum, cigarettes (I gave the cigarettes away), an address book, a photograph container and a pocket magazine. Sure was appreciated. I got all those swell Christmas packages right before I left Guam. I had to open them there because we were getting ready to shove off shortly and I couldn't carry them with me. However, I managed to save some canned goods and carried them here with me. They sure made a swell snack. Those packages sure helped to brighten my Christmas.

I hope you found that box I sent from Hawaii in good shape. Those G.I. post office boys are pretty rough. I sure hope you like the stuff. 'Tain't much but at least it's from Hawaii, which makes it novel.

Gosh, I was really glad that *(Uncle)* Pete finally got home. I bet this is the merriest Christmas he has had in a long time. He really deserves it. It goes without saying that this is the merriest Christmas for a lot of guys who've been away for a long time. I sure am glad for Pete and all of them.

Well, I gotta' quit for now. I am thinking of you and Pop and Pat and "The Runt" tonight. Please have a Merry Christmas.
My love to you all, Bunk

****

(This letter, dated Dec. 25, 1945, was inside the Christmas package Nat mailed from the Marine postal facility in Hawaii 9/24/45. It was written in Sept. in Hawaii before he packed & mailed his Christmas box. How thoughtful of an 18-yr-old to give his family's package this added touch, 3 months earlier. I include it with the December letters. It has as its signature a cartoon: Marine Nat reclining under a palm tree to which was attached, by a large nail, a Christmas stocking. He is waving to a tiny Santa & reindeer in the sky.)

Dec. 25. 1945
(Oahu, Hawaii)

Dear Folks,

Here it is Christmas again and Santa Claus holds full sway over the Wright household. It's a little different this year, though. I'm not there to break the Victrola records or knock the balls off the tree and "stuff like that there". However, don't let this take away from the joy of the occasion. I'll be thinking about you and remembering all our other Christmases. There's always a certain magic about this time of year. I remember the kick I used to get out of wandering downtown among the crowd, looking in store windows, and listening to carols, playing the Victrola when nothing but the tree lights were on, and the "Runt" on Christmas morning, and Pop snoring on the couch that night in his abbreviated shorts (that didn't hide a durn thing). Oh well, this is only a temporary absence and maybe next year I'll be home for all these things.

The stuff in this box are just a few things I picked up in Honolulu, a little sample of the tourist trade. Hope ya' like 'em. Also enclosed are a few photos taken in Honolulu. They're pretty grotesque, but at least they're me. I didn't find anything that I thought Pop would like so I asked Pat to get something to give him for me.

Well, have a good time and don't worry about me. Just write and tell me how "Sandy Claws" treated you all. Merry Christmas and a very Happy New Year.

My love to you all, Bunk

P.S. Hey, Pat! Keep your nose out of that egg nog or you'll be an old soak before your time! (And don't eat all of Mother's lemon pie before I get there).

****

Miyakonojo, Japan
(Fri.) Jan 11, 1946

Dear Mother,

Gosh, here I am, tardy again with my letter-writing. Seems as though I'm always behind. Right after Christmas, our platoon went out on a patrol and didn't get back till after the first of the year. We went by train and truck about a hundred miles west to a little-known part of Kyushu. We got off at the town of Kobyashi and went by truck to the small village of Suki, where we established quarters at an empty school house. Our routine was made up of daily treks over different trails and roads that led through grain fields and over steep, wooded hills. We searched out caves, homes and other places, looking for military property and information.

Along the way we questioned Jap civilians we met. On the whole, they were greatly afraid of us, as we were the first Marines most of them had ever seen. They had probably heard that American Marines devoured people like cannibals, so they cowered away from us wherever we went. We did, however, meet a few Jap Army and Navy veterans. We managed to get a couple of them to talk to us. On the whole, they were sullen and quiet. One told us that he had fought in California. I guess he thought we were pretty gullible. He had a Jap Okinawa campaign ribbon on his cap. On New Year's Day, the wife of our Jap interpreter fried some chicken for us. All in all, the trip proved very interesting.

As soon as our bunch got back, I was put on mess duty. Not because of anything I did. They were short-handed at the mess hall, so I was one of the "chosen". I will remain on mess duty till February 1st. Gawsh! After 2 weeks at Nagasaki and a month of it here, I oughta' make somebody a wonderful maid someday.

I sure was surprised to hear that Willie Hetrick was home so soon. Before I left Guam, I was talking to some 4th Division fellows who told me that the band had gone back to the States, but I didn't expect him to make it that fast. Please mail me his address when you can. I wrote him using his overseas address. It'll probably reach him in **1986**. Oh, by the way, do you have any idea where Dick Murphy is now? I went to look for him on Guam, but had no luck.

Hope your New Year was a happy one. I bet *(Uncle)* Pete had a rousing time. He sure deserved all the fun he could get. The free beer flowed deep New Year's Eve (so did the free Coke which pleased me no end) over here and the camp slop chute was really "yumpin" (by yiminy).

I gotta' trot back to the mess hall. Can't keep those lovely pots and trays waiting. 'Nuff for now. More later.

My love to you all, Bunk

P.S. And tell Pat please hurry and send me that picture of her sorority in sweaters that she promised. It's getting kinda' cold here and I need to keep my room warm as the stove is rather small.

****

(Usually, Nat reserved his "Tall Tales" for sister Pat. However, he obviously had nothing really interesting to write, so this "Tall Tale" is for Mother)

Miyakonojo Japan
(Tue.) Jan. 15, 1946

Dear Mother,

Ah, ecstasy of ecstasies! Today I managed to wheedle a day off from the mess hall and decided to spend it in the sack (A Marine's best friend is his sack). However, this plan soon proved to be fraught with disaster. No sooner had I jumped in and dozed off when I was rudely awakened by a loud banging and a rain of sawdust coming from above me. This was caused by a group of Nip carpenters repairing the ceiling. I got up and trudged sleepily over to the room where Bill Bridges, a buddy of mine from Mississippi, sleeps, hoping to take a snooze in his sack, as he was on guard duty today. However, he had been relieved early and was making use of it himself. I was then contemplating going over to the recreation hall, when I noticed an empty sack across the room belonging to Alex Wynstra from Wisconsin, who was also on guard duty. Still fate was against me. Just as I was ready to crawl in, in came Alex, relieved from watch, and flopped wearily on the sack. "Coises!" Foiled again!

I gave up the idea and went over to the rec hall, where I am now. Oh well, what's the use of going to sleep when you'll only wake up and get tired again? We have a pretty nice rec hall. It was made out of an old Japanese warehouse. There is a ping pong room, a library and two reading rooms. Also there is a hand-wound Victrola and records ranging from jive to "Nutcracker Suite". In the reading rooms are a lot of magazines. However, the latest issue is from around the middle of November. The library is small, but contains quite a few good books. I am now reading "Lost in the Horse Latitudes" by H. Allen Smith. It's really a riot. Down in the ping pong room is an old Jap organ, on which I have managed to pick out "Chop Sticks" and a few boogie tunes.

Oh, by the way, I'm a school boy again. For an hour a day, I attend a refresher class in English grammar in the rec hall. I am going to apply for a correspondence course in English Literature from the Marine Corps Institute in Washington. Between the two courses, I should be able to brush up considerably in preparation for starting college.

I'm slightly bruised up today. Yesterday I was playing football during some spare time I had away from the mess hall. I was playing center against a beefy brute who mauled me around considerably. I found out later that he was a former star player for the University of Southern California (Oh, my achin' back!). We played in the middle of a Jap farm and once, during an extra rough play, we got the Nip farmer slightly upset when we overturned his cart and scared his horse away (Some fun, eh kid?).

How'd Pop make out during the ducking season? I sure do miss that roast duck and cranberry sauce. I hear *(Cousin)* Bill has been having pretty good luck with the "swoose" this year. As Aunt Fanny Cockey *(Bill's mother)*, says, I guess "the goose hangs high" in the Cockey meat house. We have chicken once in a while over here, but these so-called Marine cooks don't cook 'em - they torture 'em to death.

There goes chow call so I gotta' trot off.

Love to you all, Bunk

P.S. How'd the Redskins do this year? The sports news is kinda' meager around these parts.

****

Miyakonojo, Japan
(Sat.) Jan. 19, 1946

Dear Mother,

Nothing' much doin' around here. Things have more or less settled down to a routine of guard duty, patrols, a few working details and, once in a while, a parade. Being as I am on mess duty, I have managed to miss these duties but after February 1st, I'll fall right in with the schedule.

We got paid yesterday. Since we have moved around considerably since we were last paid, my pay stacked up quite a bit. I drew $110, or 1650 yen. They pay us in Japanese money. We can't use American money here. And on top of everything, there's hardly anything to buy in town. So here I am with 1650 yen I drew in pay (which is more than a captain in the Jap army got in three months) plus 450 yen (30 dollars) I had on hand (which I acquired by selling cigarettes to the Japs for over a dollar a pack when I was hard up for cash after the fire at Nagasaki), the grand total coming to 2100 yen.

However, being as there isn't much to buy (and gosh knows I'll never need all that dough), I've decided for once in my life to do something sensible with my money. I have put in an application to send $110 home for you and Pop to put in the bank for me. It's about time I started looking ahead and saving some of my dough. After all, I won't always be in the Marine Corps. Someday I'll be on my own. Also, I'd better save some to supplement the G.I. bill of rights in regard to college. I'm going to send part of my pay home each month to be deposited in the bank. Sure sounds odd for me to be saving money, doesn't it? Well, weird things will happen, you know.

I hope everyone has gotten over that flu epidemic that spread over the household. Our family sure is popular with the flu. Remember that Christmas we all had it?

Gosh, I'd sure like to see the "Runt" now. The last time I saw her she was just getting into the colt stage when her legs seemed to be stretching out. I bet she's really springing up. It's hard to realize she's almost 6. It's also hard to visualize Pat as a senior. Hold on now! This is no knock to Patricia's mentality (which I have knocked many times, as you doubtless remember). It just seems that time has gone by so fast since she was a front-toothless squirt that used to tie my shoes for me when we went to elementary school.

As for me, I feel fine. I haven't been bothered by colds so far. It's pretty cold here but we've had no real snowfall, just a few snow flurries. However, it's pretty windy and rainy.

I've gained a little weight and, surprise of surprises, I have grown a little, too. Zig, my buddy from Minnesota, measured me the other day and, according to his measurements, I'm an even 5 feet 7. Gigantic, what? *(I told you he would lie about his height!)*

I better quit for now. This Nip pen is leaking all over my fingers. And besides, I'll just have time to drop this in the box before the mail goes out.

My love to you all, Bunk

****

Miyakonojo, Japan
(Thu.) Jan. 24, 1946

Dear Mother,

Today I was relieved from mess duty for a few hours in order to go out to the newly-completed rifle range about seven miles from here. The reason I had to go there was to "zero" (test fire) my rifle. My old one burned up at Nagasaki so I had to test out my new one today. We went on foot, but I didn't mind that as it gave me a chance to see more of the Jap countryside and rural life. Also, the sun was out pretty bright and it was one of the warmest days we've had all winter. So, all in all, it was fairly pleasant. On the way, we passed the wreckage of several Jap planes in the middle of a field.

When I got back, I was told that the C.O. has approved my application to send 110 dollars home to be placed in the bank. So I went to the post office and got a money order which I am enclosing with this letter.

One of the fellows in my company has devised a football game with dice similar to the "Elmer Laydon" game I have at home. Several of us recently held a tournament. We all "anted" in a pot, winner getting two thirds and runner-up getting one third. I won 50 yen (a little over $3). Not bad for a guy who was never much good in games of chance.

Is *(Cousin)* Dinny still in Illinois or has he been transferred? The last I heard *(Cousin)* Sud was in Manila. Gosh, we sure are scattered. I sure do miss the farm gang.

How long does it take my letters to reach you from here? I hope that you are receiving them with some amount of regularity. The mail must still be fouled up to a certain extent. The day before yesterday I received two Christmas packages, one from you and one from Mrs. Carter. They sure were swell and were greatly appreciated. I immediately became popular with these ever-hungry chow hounds I live with over here. Thanks a lot.

'Nuff for now. Chow time!

My love to you all, Bunk

****

Miyakonojo, Japan
(Sun.) Jan. 27, 1946

Dear Pat,

Hee-yer I ay-um, yuk yuk, with a few hours before I have to trot back to the mess hall, so I thought it's about time I scrawled off a letter to you. Mess duty over here is a better deal than back in the States. They're not so particular about the decks and walls, etc. being spic and span. Also, they're a lot more lenient with the mess men. We're always grabbing little snacks here and there between meals. The mess hall is in a building that used to house a Jap laundry. At one end is a row of large cast iron vats, about three feet each in diameter and about two and ½ feet deep. They were formerly used by the Nips for dirty clothes, but we use them for washing pots and trays, which is my job. Woe is me! I'm getting dish pan hands up to the elbows. Three other fellows and I wash the trays and four Japs wash the pots. The pots require the most work and the hardest scrubbing, so the Japs do them. The tray-washing job is pretty simple.

We have Nips around to do the dirty jobs like sweeping, garbage handling, etc. We are always clowning around with the four Nips who wallop the pots. So far, we have taught them "Auld Lang Syne", "You Are My Sunshine" and "The Marines' Hymn", and now we are teaching the Miyakonojo Minstrels, as we call them, "Pistol Packin' Mama". At present, I have undertaken the project of teaching them a burlesque dancing routine which includes the customary kicking and throwing-around of the appropriate anatomy. They got a buzz out of one certain bump involving the hips and other local areas. In return they have been showing me a couple of simple Japanese dances. Not very sexy, though.

In one of my last letters, I think I told you about Nagasaki. So now I'll tell you something about Miyakonojo, which ain't much. To begin with, I'd like to correct a geographical error I made about this place in one of my recent letters. I said that it was in North Central Kyushu, which was a rough guess. Well, today I got hold of a map of Kyushu which showed Miyakonojo to be at the southern end of Kyushu about 30 miles from the coast at its nearest point.

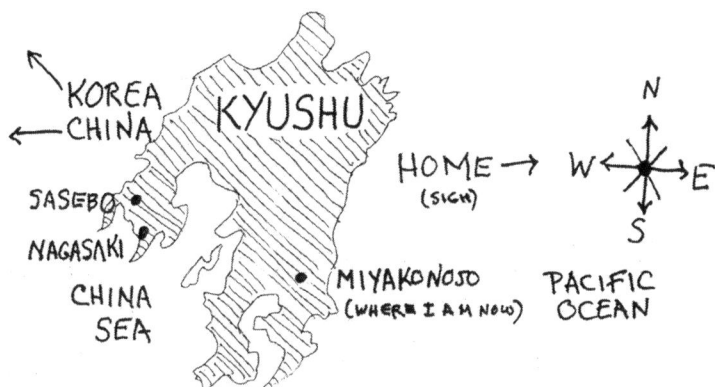

And now you have some idea of where I am. When I first got here, I didn't know where I was. For all I knew, I might have been in Upper Marlboro. Then I heard someone mention the name "Miyakonojo". It sounded like the name of a cigar store Indian from Yugoslavia. However, it turned out to be the name of the joint.

It's a fairly good-sized town, sort of a doubled "Frederick Town" with two (think of it, two!) horse troughs and <u>two</u> "cone-houses" instead of one each (big time!). The place was bombed but not very heavily. However, there was right much damage done on the north side of town where the railroad station and the lumber & freight yards are (Pardon the messiness of this page. So far it has been knocked off the table twice by my roughneck buddies). The main trade carried on in town is done in small, shabby shops. However, their stocks are small and their wares are simple. They sell such nick-nacks as fans, purses, chop sticks, etc. Also, they sell a few articles of clothing and some household articles. I have picked up a few trinkets. I'm going to try to send some stuff home. You have to go through a lot of red tape to send stuff home from here.

There are a couple of Jap movie theaters in town. I have been to a couple of shows just for the novelty of it, not that I understand what the blazes they're talking about on the screen. They all sound like Cliff Nazzarro, the double-talk artist. I get a kick out of the pantomime and facial expressions. Of course the plot is a bit thick, but one can determine different moods. It seems there's always a sad note to each story. Some poor soul is always kicking the bucket and there's nearly always a big funeral scene which involves a lot of pageantry. This includes a lot of weird chants and dances, colorful costumes and the waving of huge lanterns and standards. Also, no matter what the story may be, there's a lot of bowing. In all pictures, whenever two characters meet, they always greet each other with low bows. Sloan's Liniment would do a landslide business here because, with all the bowing, chronic back aches must be quite the vogue.

Miyakonojo is located in a long, fairly wide valley surrounded by blue-gray hills and mountains. The valley floor is level but the hills and mountains are very steep. There is one mountain that juts up into the clouds. Its peak can be seen only on very clear days. This is Mount Kirishima. The valley is divided into small farms. The Nip farmers live and work crudely, but they are, on the whole, very tidy. Each small field is bordered either by a low hedge row or a neat, grassy ridge. Farmers very seldom terrace the hillsides around here, as they do around Nagasaki, because there is more level land around these parts. The land around Nagasaki is nearly all hills.

The Japs have quite an unusual way of celebrating New Years. They put on their best clothes and nearly every family gets out and builds a new fence in front of their house. However, this year very few could afford new fences, but all of them put on their "Sunday-go-to-meetin' " clothes. The men wore clothes of the same style as men's fashions in the States and the women were bedecked in their brightest kimonos.

Well, how are things progressing in the old "Inner Sanctum"? I guess you're preparing for the home stretch of "ye olde" eighth semester. *(Pat would graduate with the class of June, 1946.)* I sure miss the old crematory. Remember the paper menagerie we brought home from your Junior Prom? My, but that was ga-a-ay. *(That did not then have the connotation it now has.)* By the way, how did the school team finally make out? The last word I heard about them was after the Central game.

The mail must still be fouled up. The last letter I got was dated December 14th. I hope they get deliveries straightened out soon. I'm starved for news from home.

Time to whip on back to the mess hall. So long for now.

Love, Nat

****

Miyakonojo, Japan
(Fri.) Feb. 8, 1946

Dear Mother,

Right much has happened since I last wrote. To begin with, the big boss gave me a raise. I'm now a PFC. Whattya' know! In a matter of a mere 75 years or so, I may be a brigadier general. Also, our battalion is getting ready to break up. Soon I'll be transferred to either the first or second battalion of the 2nd Marines. Dad-rat it! That will mean another foul-up of the mail situation. There must be something about me that inspires deterioration. Every outfit I get into busts up. I will more than likely be sent either to Miyazaki, about 50 miles northeast of here, or to Beppu, up near the north side of Kyushu. Gawsh, guess I'll never get settled. The breaking-up is scheduled to start Monday, February 11th.

Sunday three of my buddies and I went horseback riding. I really got a kick out of it (not to mention, a very sore - uh - pride). We rode through rice paddies in the valley, where we occasionally saw some Jap farmers threshing out shocks of rice. Most of them were beating the bundles with crude clubs with knobs on the end. However, there were a couple who were using a small machine with a spiked roller, somewhat like a crude cotton gin, operated by a foot pedal. Through the center of the valley runs a narrow, shallow river that twists and winds crazily. We crossed it and rode up into the foot hills. We passed through several small villages. Hordes of kids trailed after us yelling "chooeen gum!" We rode along the ridges and got a swell panorama view of the valley.

The other fellows had pretty good horses, but you know me - I had to draw a plug. The nag I was riding must have been either a Bing Crosby cast-off or a fugitive from a glue factory. When we got back, I felt like a cross between a pair of pliers and a cocktail shaker. Well, anyway I had a lot of fun even at the cost of a sadly flailed flank.

I sure was surprised to hear that *(Cousin)* Dinny is in Puerto Rico. What is his job? I'm glad that *(Uncle)* Pete is finally getting to go to Hopkins. He really has waited long enough.

Well, 's getting kinda late, so I better quit for now. More later.

Love to you all, Bunk

P.S. I just got the word from the top sergeant that I'm being transferred to the 2nd battalion. It should be about a week or so before I leave.

****

Miyakonojo, Japan
(Wed.) Feb. 13, 1946

Dear Mother,

I'm still standing by to leave. In a couple of days I will be transported to the 2nd battalion, which, as far as I know, is at Beppu, somewhere north of here. A large group of fellows has already left to join the 1st battalion at Miyazaki. The 3rd battalion, where I am now, will be made up of men with 45 points and will be sent home along with high-point men of the other regiments of the 2nd Division. I guess my routine in the 2nd battalion will be much the same as it was here, guard duty, patrols, etc.

I wrote to Hal Wood's mother and got his address. He's in a Signal company at Sasebo. His job is riding around in a truck climbing poles (not in the truck, of course) and installing wires.

A couple of days ago I went into town on liberty. While I was moseying around I wandered into a small, dusty shop. The wares were few, the stock consisting mainly of a few household articles, pieces of clothing, and a few Jap toilet articles. The shop keeper was a small, round-shouldered, buck-toothed old codger who spoke pretty good English. He was a pretty friendly guy and he invited me to the rear of his shop. At first I was cautious as Japs seem to have acquired a reputation for not being very trustworthy. However, I consented to go, figuring that if any trouble started I could bash the old boy in his front choppers and take off. He nevertheless proved harmless and very friendly. I followed him to the rear of the shop to a small flooring slightly elevated on a platform about two feet higher than the rest of the shop floor.

We removed our shoes (I took off my G.I. boondockers and he slipped off his wooden sandals) and squatted Indian-style on little woven mats. He offered me tea in a little cup the size of a shot glass. I asked him questions about Kyushu, nearby towns, the people, the location of laundries in town and other stuff. I also learned some more words and phrases in Japanese. Then, after buying a woven handbag and giving a stick of gum to his runny-nosed kid, who stood around gaping and sucking his thumb, I left and took a bundle of my dirty clothes to a laundry he recommended. It was really an enjoyable experience.

I am enclosing a money order for 50 dollars to be deposited in the bank. This plus the 110 dollars I sent before ought to make a pretty good start for a savings account. I hope I can keep on sending part of my pay home. There's no reason why I shouldn't be able to because there's nothing useful to spend money on over here, so the best bet is for me to send it home to be deposited. Odd for me (Old Castor Oil Charlie) to be saving dough, ain't it?

I gotta trot off now as some of my buddies are waiting for me to go to a movie with them. Lana Turner is showing tonight (and I do mean <u>showing</u>!).

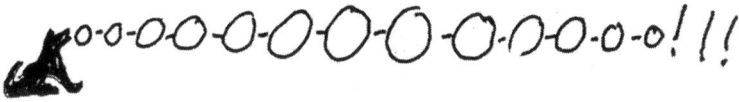

o-o-oo-o-o-o-o-o-o-o-o-o-o!!!

S'long for now,
Love to you all, Bunk

✱✱✱✱

Miyakonojo, Japan
(Sun.) Feb. 17, 1946

Dear Mother,

Here I wait still. We have been told that we will leave for the 2nd battalion any day now. You know how unpredictable this outfit is. At any rate we should move out before long.

I have prepared a large box of Jap souvenirs to send home. I packed a Jap rifle, a bayonet, two swords, a couple of fans, several wooden miniatures, a pair of woven sandals and a little bamboo cigarette holder. The box is now in the company commander's office waiting for his O.K. After he approves it, I can mail it. It'll take pretty long for the box to get home, probably about two months. I hope it makes it O.K. *(It did. The rifle, 1 sword & a fan remain in the family's possession.)*

Some of my back mail has been catching up with me. I sure was surprised to hear that Aunt Fanny Wright is expecting the stork. I, too, hope it's a girl. Tell "Cuzzin" Les that sisters aren't so bad. They kinda' grow on you (to which he will probably say, "Yeah, so do warts."). I wish I had known that Uncle Les & Co. were going to be with you on Christmas as I would have included something in that Christmas box for them. "Anyhoo", even if it is a bit late, wish them a Merry Christmas, Happy New Year, Good Luck an' stuff like that there for me. And tell little Les I'll write him soon.

Alex and Zig and a couple more of my buddies are yelling for me to go take a shower with them, so I gotta' run. Enclosed is a handkerchief I got in town. Hope you like it.

Love, Bunk

****

Miyakonojo, Japan
Feb. 22nd, 1946

Dear Pat,

Tomorrow we shove off for the 2nd battalion of the 2nd regiment. We train for Oita ("Oh-ee-ta"), about a hundred or so miles north of here on the northeast corner of Kyushu. The trip will take about ten hours.

The January issue of the Pow Wow arrived yesterday. The GMA is riding high. Gotta' hand it to you gals - you're really progressing. The school paper seems to be getting bigger and better. Oi! Photographs, yet!

Well, I gotta get packed so I better quit for now. I'll write as soon as I get settled.

I'm enclosing a handkerchief for you. I hope you like it.

Cheese 'n crackers! Gotta ' hurry, so-o-o-o-

Sayonara (Goodbye),

Nat

****

Oita, Japan
(Sun.) Feb. 24, 1946

Dear Pat,

We arrived here this morning after a 10-hour train ride from Miyakonojo. Boy, what a brutal train ride it was! We traveled in dirty, drafty coaches that looked like street cars salvaged from the San Francisco earthquake. I slept or, that is, attempted to sleep, in every imaginable position. Not that I was cramped, but when we got here I could scratch my left ear with my right foot (Just like those gay rollicking days on the 17th & Penna. Car).

Our camp is located at the edge of Oita, a good-sized seaport town located on the very northeast corner of Kyushu. The place was hit pretty hard a couple of times. However, the better part of it is still in pretty fair condition. About seven miles up the coast is Beppu (Bep-poo) where we can go on liberty. Beppu, from all reports, is a large, pretty town, practically unscathed by bombs. In fact, some say it was untouched by bombs, which should be a novelty, as most of the places I've seen have been a bombed-out mess except for a few smaller towns like Miyakonojo, Suki, Kobyashi, etc.

Oita is out of bounds for troops because of widespread disease. The only reason we are located here is because there are better quarters afforded than at any other place in the vicinity. We are quartered in former Jap garrison barracks like the ones at Miyakonojo.

Also quartered in parts of this camp is the 120th field artillery battalion of the 32nd Army division, the only "doggie" division on Kyushu. They are moving out soon and this place will be run totally by Marines.

The 2nd battalion of the 2nd Marines seems to be a lot better than the 3rd Battalion. They're not nearly so strict on us and the facilities are a lot better up here. I am now in F Co., commonly referred to as "Fox" Co. Each company in a line outfit is given a phonetic or nick name to correspond with its letter. For example: A Co is "Able" Co. B Co. is "Baker" (or sometimes "Beaver") Co. C Co. is "Charlie" Co., etc. In the 3rd Battalion, I was in "King" Co. Now I'm in "Fox" Co. (or should that be Wolf Co.?).

I gotta hit the sack as I'm pretty pooped.

"Fox" Co, 'tenshun! Sack time, march!

Fall out! (thud!) **Love, Nat**

＊＊＊＊

Oita, Japan
(Fri.) March 8, 1946

Dear Mother,

Here I go getting lazy again. I've no excuse. I guess I just let it slide. The weather here hasn't proved very inspirational to letter-writing. It has rained most all the time since I got here from Miyakonojo. Oita is right on the sea coast and a pretty long stretch of wet weather hits here about this time of year. Quite often an icy wind comes whipping in off the water and really lets us know that it's March.

It's been pretty cold here this winter but we've had practically no snow. What little snow we've had has come in brief, windy flurries, usually followed by rain. From all reports you must really be having some heavy winter weather back there. I saw a picture in a magazine of Capitol Hill enveloped in snow. Sure looked good.

Oita is a large, dingy seaport town inhabited mostly by fishermen. Beppu, a city about seven miles up the coast, is where we go on liberty. There's a "Toonerville" trolley that runs from Oita to Beppu. It runs right along the coast. The land around here much resembles the land around Sasebo and Nagasaki - steep hills that jut sharply up. Many hillsides are terraced. There are also many orange groves around here.

On one of the few sunny days we've had lately, I went on liberty with Milt Gillespie, a buddy of mine from Macon, Ga. We boarded the trolley and started on the rocky, twisty track to Beppu. The line runs right along the seashore. There are steep hills and ridges that shoot right up out of the water. At some places, the trolley is almost crowded off into the ocean. There were droves of wild ducks along the shore. A shot gun would have been handy then. I sure miss those duck dinners.

Beppu is nestled in a little valley overlooking the ocean. On either side of the city are steep, high, pine-covered hills. Directly in back, a short way inland, is a lofty, snow-capped mountain. We got off the trolley at the waterfront. Beppu and Oita are situated in a small inlet called Beppu Wan. The ocean is comparatively calm here. There were many fishing boats at the docks and along the waterfront were many fish markets (phew!) and grog shops (which are out of bounds). We proceeded up the town's main commercial street. We browsed through various and sundry small shops. The shops in Beppu are on the whole much tidier and more up to date than the ones at Miyakonojo and have a bigger and better variety of wares.

Beppu generally is about the cleanest and prettiest Japanese town I've seen so far. It is a typical example of an Oriental city. The streets, except for the main commercial drag and the waterfront street, are narrow. The houses, although most are two stories high, are squatty and have wide, gently sloping, tile roofs with wide eaves that almost touch, on some streets, with the eaves of the house on the other side. There are noisy market places and people busily klip-klopping here and there on wooden sandals. Also, there are droves of laughing, dirty-faced little kids playing with tops and yo-yos. Really an interesting town and the first place we've been that hasn't been hit by bombs. We spent the day just wandering around looking the place over.

I guess you've probably noticed that so far I haven't speculated in any of my letters as to when I expect to be home. Well, for quite a while there has been a lot of scuttlebutt and the rumors have been many and varied. So I never brought the subject up for fear of raising false hopes or something to that effect. However, some reliable dope came out in the 2nd Division newspaper recently that all Marine reserves and selective service men are expected to be home by September. The only Marines expected to be in Japan after September are the regulars (four-year men). Even so, September seems like a pretty good way off, but I haven't much cause to complain as quite a few of my buddies are vets of Iwo Jima and Okinawa and have been over here nearly two years. I missed all the fireworks and have been overseas only seven months, so I've gotta wait my turn for that Stateside boat.

We have settled down to the usual routine of guard duty and patrols. The only big rub is the wet weather. Reminds me of Camp Lejeune last summer, only the rain over here is much chillier.

I feel O.K. and can't kick, I hope you all are doin' fine.

Well almost time for chow so I gotta run. More soon.

Love to you all, Bunk

****

(A combination letter to Pat: factual information & at least one "Tall Tale".)

Oita, Japan
(Fri.) March 15, 1946

Dear Pat,

Konnichiwa! Gokigen wa ikaga deska? Watakshi wa yoku shite imas. Tenki koko warui des.
 Good day! *How are you?*   *I am well.*   *The weather here is lousy.*

Tabemono koko joto ori-ori des. Sho-I watakshi-tachi-no kitsu oki shite des. Gomen Nasai!
 The chow here is occasionally good. *Our second lieutenants are big CENSOREDs.* *Excuse me!*

Benjo oitoma seneba nari-masen ......(cucho) ..... Ah! ..... kiyasme okina!
 I must go to the head.   ...... *(pause)* ..... *Ah!* ..... *Great relief!*

Honest, that's what it says. I've been here long enough now to have picked up a few basic terms, phrases, words, etc. so as to enable me to be better understood. However, if that paragraph in Japanese were broken down verbatim by a Japanese teacher, it would probably prove to be very crude and simple. Nevertheless, a Jap could understand it. I am trying to pick up as many terms as I can. It would take years of study to really learn this language. Also, that paragraph I wrote is the verbal or spoken Japanese. Cheese 'n crackers, it'd take a couple of lifetimes to learn how to write the stuff. Here's a small example of written Japanese:

(a line of Japanese characters)

Translation: (Nat Wright) (Washington)

Confoozin', ain't it?

Right before I left Miyakonojo, I mailed a box of souvenirs home. In it were a Jap rifle, a Jap bayonet, two Jap N.C.O. swords, six bamboo miniatures, two fans, a bamboo cigarette holder, two souvenir Jap flags, and a pair of small hand woven sandals. *(The rifle, 1 Samurai sword & 1 fan remain in the family's possession.)* Miyakonojo didn't have much in the way of souvenir trinkets. I looked all over for a doll for Bonnie but could find none. Those woven sandals are for her birthday. However, I promise the Runt a doll if I have to turn Beppu inside out to find one. An interpreter told me that they make pretty dolls around here (No, you sharp character, you! In this case I'm referring to <u>toys</u>!).

On a couple of the few clear days we've had recently, I've been going on liberty to Beppu with Milt Gillespie, a buddy from Georgia. Here's a bit of description about him: He's 19, tall & well built (a shade over 6 feet and about 180 lbs.), has curly brown hair, is an excellent dancer, likes Charlie Spivak, football, baseball, hunting, fried chicken and pickled peaches. He is good at judo (the thug! Oh, my sad, achin' frame!), boxed in the golden gloves tournament, went to the University of Georgia two years and played football on the same team with Frank Sinkwich, the all-American. Some lug, eh?

We always have a gay *(The word did not then have the connotation it now has.)* time (slight pause for two snaps of the fingers over each shoulder) in town together. The other day we rented jinrickshas and went for a spin around the town. We went zipping down those narrow streets bowling over pedestrians. However, I happened to miss one so I made the Nip pulling mine go back and try again.

We then staged a race. The Nip pulling my jinrikisha must have worked for Crosby at one time, as Milt went roaring by, the Jap pulling his carriage looking like Glen Cunningham compared to mine, who was loping pokily along at the speed of a peg-legged amoeba. Milt was looking back and laughing at me, but his glory was short-lived, as his driver (or should I say puller) stubbed his toe and barely averted cleaving through a vegetable stand, so we called the sweepstakes off. We gave the two Nips a couple of yen and shoved off for the Tachibana dance hall.

The Tachibana dance hall is built out on a concrete pier extending over the bay front. It is in one of Beppu's tallest buildings (four stories! Gad! What exhilarating altitude!) The inside of the joint is fixed up attractively with drapes, varnished floors and a wide window front overlooking the water. There are about 40 Jap girls acting as hostesses, dressed in loud, multicolored silk dresses. All of them can dance pretty good. They were taught by the Nip who owns the joint, who was schooled by American & European dancing teachers. The gals can handle a waltz, fox trot, etc., but the fellows really stump 'em on jitterbugging.

I spent most of the time watching Milt, who took great delight in whirling the girls around, getting them good and dizzy, and walking off, leaving them to stagger off by themselves. The jernt is equipped with a loudspeaker that plays American swing & hillbilly tunes and a few Spanish pieces. At night, the music department is handled by a six-piece Jap band that tries hard to play jazz, but sounds more like the Hoosier Hot Shots with a hangover. The fellows have named the band Sad Saki Sam's Sewage Sextet. Those little Nip girls try pretty hard to act like the Stateside gals, but they don't have much appeal for me.

You have undoubtedly heard stories about Americans fraternizing in a pretty disgusting manner with Japanese girls. Well, I've seen quite a bit of it here and there. As for me, I definitely can't see it and neither can Milt or Alex or Zig or Woj and quite a few of my buddies.

I'm no Fauntleroy, just an average guy. But we've been given the scoop on the disease rate around here (venereal and otherwise) and common sense ought to tell q guy to stay away from them. The utmost in health precautions is being done by the doctors and corpsmen but a lot of fellows still chase after these girls. Oh, there are quite a few contributing reasons. A lot of the fellows have been overseas quite a while and have seen combat and just don't give a damn. Then, of course, there are a few young chicks my age who try to act like B.T.O. *(Big Time Operators)* and do foolish things they're sorry for later.

There are three main classes of Jap women: the ojosans (the domestic working girl), the geishas (the entertainers, singers, dancers, etc.) and the joros (the prostitutes). All the joros and most of the geishas are the ones we've been warned by the "docs" about and who will - uh - "fraternize". Well, anyway, I for one am gonna stay clear of them. Well, enough of this prattling.

How're things comin' along at ye olde "Alma Tomater"? I sure miss the old stockade. Now that you're headin' down the pay dirt stretch of your senior year, I bet they've got you fairly hopping, getting ready for class day, prom, an' stuff like that there. The preparations are a big part of the fun.

Have you elected class officers yet? How're the gal commandos shaping up? (in a military sense, that is. I'm aware of the other development. Hubba-hubba!). The G.M.A. has really advanced this year. How's the Cadet battalion doing? The fellows should be ready for battalion drill about now, I guess.

I'll just have time for a shower before chow so I better quit now. Mo' latuh (as Milt would say).

I am enclosing one of our division patches. There are two designs for the patch. However they are almost identical except for a slight difference in the shape of the torch. The one I'm sending you is of the newer design. The 2nd is known as the Arrowhead Division (indicated by the shape of the patch).

You will also find enclosed a picture of Milt and me taken in a Beppu studio (The warden let us take our numbers off).

I gotta trot off now.

Love, Nat

****

Oita, Japan
(Sun.) March 24, 1946

Dear Mother,

It's getting warmer now and spring shouldn't be very far away. We are still having a lot of rain, though, and it's pretty muddy around here. A Nip interpreter told me that the summers are pretty warm here. I'll sure be glad to see warm weather as it'll be more pleasant standing guard duty.

I'm writing this in our Red Cross recreation hall. It's one of the best rec halls I've seen over here. It is located in a two-wing Jap building. In one wing is a barber shop, tailor shop and PX. The barbers and tailors are Japs. I've had all my shirts cut down. The ones they issued me after the Nagasaki fire fitted me like tents.

Well, getting back to the rec hall, in the other wing is what we call our "crap-out" room. Inside are several Nip sofas & upholstered chairs, a piano, a ping pong table and a doughnut and coffee bar that serves 'em as long as you can down 'em (free! hoot mon!). It's better than the rec hall at Miyakonojo, which was run by Marine Special Services. The hall up here is run by the Red Cross, which has better equipment and doesn't have to go through as much red tape as Marine Special Services. The Red Cross is going to open a place in Beppu. I hear there might be a couple of American Red Cross girls there (hubba hubba!). The place here in camp is run by an R.C. field director, aided by Marine and Japanese help.

The mail from home is coming through a little better now and the news is a little more recent. I sure am sorry to hear about the Runt's front teeth. Does she go around saying, "Uncle Thud's *(Uncle Sud)* a hunka' cheeth", too?

Enclosed you will find a money order for $15 to be banked. I intended to send more but a buddy of mine was in a rut for some dough so I lent him some.

I go on guard in half an hour so I better quit for now.

Love to you all, Bunk

****

Oita, Japan
(Thu.) March 28, 1946

Dear Mother,

I have just come from our new movie hall. The camp facilities have been improved lately with the opening of a new movie hall and slop chute (beer hall, remember?). Here, as at Miyakonojo, we are living in former Japanese garrison barracks. They also have been improved with the addition of new showers. So we can't beef much in the way of quarters. I went out to the battalion rifle range to test-fire my B.A.R. (Browning Automatic Rifle). They recently issued me this when the high-pointer it belonged to went home. It has received pretty rough treatment as its former owner carried it on Okinawa. However, it still makes a loud bang and shoots pretty straight, so it'll do O.K.

The civilian food supply is getting low over here. The guard has been increased at several G.I. warehouses full of chow and PX gear. The chief cause of the scarcity is an intricate civilian black market that keeps a lot of food off the regular grocery stands. The high brass had better straighten it out pretty quick as I have seen some pretty sick little kids. And whether they be Japanese, American or Scotch-Armenian, I don't like to see sick kids. The G.I. chow stock just covers our needs so we can't draw on that for civilian needs. The Nip farms are supplying right much produce, but the black market ties up distribution to the consumer. Our battalion has been alerted for civilian food riots. Each day one platoon from each company acts as a riot squad and stands by with combat equipment for immediate call in case of trouble. My platoon gets the riot squad duty about once a week. There have been no riots as yet. Our company has guard duty every other day.

Yesterday I went to Beppu. I felt in a roving mood, so I just wandered around. I went into a Jap school on the northern edge of town. All the grades from kindergarten through high school are in the same building. It is a long two-story building of several wings with a flowery courtyard between each wing. It was during recess and most of the kids were out on the playground playing baseball (a Jap favorite), spinning tops, etc.

I first went through part of the high school. I was surprised to find several well-equipped biology and chemistry labs. Then I went upstairs to the primary grades. I passed several empty rooms, inside of which were tiny desks and chairs. At the end of the hall was what appeared to be a music room. Inside were some tiny drums, castanets, cymbals, tambourines and a small piano.

I went into a kindergarten classroom around the corner from the music room. The teacher wasn't there, but the room was full of little tots about half way up to my hip. They were all girls as the boys have their own separate class. I don't know why they weren't out on the playground. They were just sitting at their little desks chattering like kids will do. At first they just sat and gaped at me in silence. So I wiggled my ears and went "BOO!", which must have broken the ice as they started giggling and went "BOO!" right back.

I sat down on one of their little desks and showed them the pictures in my wallet of the gang at home, some of my buddies here, and a couple I had taken in a Pearl Harbor photo stand (like the ones I sent you). They got the biggest kick out of my identification picture and one of those Hawaii photos of me and a gal. They were always giggling. I don't know whether they were laughing at me, the pictures, or poking fun at me because I never went to kindergarten. They were cute little shavers, dressed in little blue middies & slacks and all had those straight bowl haircuts and bangs. When I left they all giggled and yelled "Sayonara" (pronounced: "Sah-yoh-nah-rah", meaning "goodbye"). I sure got a bang out of it.

I got that card with holes of different ring sizes on it that you sent me. However, I misplaced it somewhere (as I am always doing). So I'll enclose a piece of string indicating the circumference of my finger.

Tonight at the movie hall, before the picture started, we were entertained with a piano concert by an Italian missionary from the Order of Silesian Priests. He is 67 years old, has been in Japan 21 years, and has a white beard nearly to his waist. He played and sang "Ave Maria" (very well for an old guy), a couple of Straus waltzes, and rendered "Santa Lucia" with so much gusto that the hind leg of the Nip piano gave way and the concert was delayed for repairs. The fellows gave him a big hand.

There's taps - gotta hit the sack now.

Love to you all,
and Kombanwa (good night),
Bunk

****

(Written to Mother after a lengthy hiatus, as he had been out on a long patrol, this was the longest letter Nat wrote during his entire Marine hitch & perhaps the most lyrical. He was always fascinated with his surroundings & the inhabitants & loved to write about them.)

Oita, Japan

(Mon.) April 15, 1946

Dear Mother,

Oi! Another gap in my letter writing! However, this time I think I can offer a plausible excuse. I just returned yesterday from a nine-day patrol. And what a patrol, the best and the most eventful I've been on yet!

We boarded a train and after a two-hour ride, we pulled into Takeda, a small town in the mountains about 70 miles from here. Takeda is about the size of Stevensville *(The small town near the farm where Nat spent his summers & many holidays w/ his cousins, & where we were eventually married.)*, only the houses are grouped more closely. It is situated in a basin formed by steep, rocky bluffs which lie on three sides. Several small waterfalls plunge off the crests of the bluffs and run in quick little streamlets to the Kujyu Gawa, a narrow, rapid river that flows right thru the town. We hit that neck of the country just when the cherry blossoms were at their peak and it really was beautiful to see them all over the terraced hills on the bluffs, and down in the valley. These people take great pride in their cherry blossoms. Each year about this time they hold a big festival.

Takeda is a typical small Jap town, only cleaner than most. There is a comparatively wide main drag, but the rest of its streets are extremely narrow. The houses are mostly of two stories - even so they are squat. They are constructed of very light material and, except for some few of the shops, have paneled, sliding doors and windows. Most of the doors and windows are covered with translucent paper as few can afford plate glass.

The main drag is pretty busy during the day. There are farmers bringing cartloads of produce into the markets, people riding bikes and klip-klopping here and there on sandals and, as usual, regiments of kids. Spring is here and most all of the women and girls are turning out in multi-colored kimonos. Some few of the women occasionally wear a short-skirted dress fashioned after Western hemisphere styles, but this is considered very risqué by most Japs. Nearly all of the men and boys still wear pieces of Jap army clothing as new clothes are very scarce.

Our patrol stayed in the town's best hotel. It is one of the few concrete buildings in Takeda and the only hotel possessing an electric sign (which didn't work but was nonetheless decorative). In conformity with Nipponese tradition, we removed our shoes before entering. The floors are covered with a woven matting, and the doors consist of sliding fiber board panels. We slept four men to a room. The rooms are small but tidy. The walls are done in pastel shades and there are small shelves on one side. On some walls are long scrolls with pictures and characters on them. On chilly days the rooms are heated by means of charcoal crocks. In the center of the hotel is a small patio with a skinny boxwood tree growing right in the middle of a shallow little pond. Enough about the hotel.

The platoon was split into three patrolling groups. The patrols were made in Nip trucks. We walked to places inaccessible by truck. I was in Group II and so was Alex Wynstra, my buddy from Wisconsin. A Marine intelligence man was attached to each group. The S-2 (intelligence) man in our group was Sam Houston (descended from the famous general). He's from D.C., where he attended Roosevelt, Central and Tech High schools .

Our job was to canvass the towns and farms, etc. for military equipment and to gain information vital to the intelligence department. Each of the three groups was given a separate area to cover. Our first afternoon there, after getting off the train and getting settled in the hotel, we were briefed by our lieutenant and the S-2 men and were given all the preliminary data. The next morning we started out early.

One of the fellows in the platoon volunteered to do the cooking. He did fine. We ate breakfast at the hotel. After putting away about a ton of eggs and bacon, we grabbed our rifles, threw some C rations on the truck and started off. Our driver was a bandy-legged, stocky Jap named Yagi, who was plenty good at wrestling with that truck on those snaky mountain roads. He was an amiable character for a Nip. He was always grinning through gold buck teeth (middle front tooth missing) and singing Japanese songs in a high-pitched, wavering voice. He proved to be very dependable.

We went out of the southwestern end of town and drove along the banks of the Kujyi Gawa for a short distance, then cut southward. After passing thru three tunnels that cut through high hills, the road began to grade upward. All about us were small farms, terraced step-like fields and patch quilt paddies on the valley floors. Nearly all of the farmhouses were constructed on the same lines, low, one-storied affairs with high, thick straw-thatched roofs. Some of the more prosperous farmers had tile roofs.

We began to climb higher and the road started to take on a course resembling that of the Burma Road. The truck was whining and straining, but we forged on steadily. We'd be heading in one direction one minute, then go zooting around a ridge and be heading the opposite way. There were countless rapid little mountain streams splashing and rippling here and there. The Nip farmers make good use of these. They use them mainly for irrigation and milling purposes. On some of the larger streams were big mill wheels.

Gawsh, I sure wish you could have been with me to take in that mountain scenery. It really was something to behold. Riding along those high roads, you could look down a flight of green, grain-filled steps to a rocky, deep-cut ravine where a swift, narrow river flows. From up where we were, the river looked like a silver ribbon. Cedar-covered mountains jutted up all around us. There were also plenty of cherry blossoms.

Our first stop was at a little mountain village whose name was larger than the town. The town contained a pretty large school and several small warehouses. We searched these and found a few various and sundry military articles. Americans had only passed through the town once before, but we were the first to search it out. The people stood timidly by and gaped. Whenever we approached or spoke to them, they bowed low like Arabs facing the east. Alex and I approached a storage house in back of a farmer's house. It was locked so I asked a shaven-headed little boy who was standing nearby, "Anata-no-ottosan dokodeska"? ("Where is your father"?). He whirled around, flew toward the house, tripping over a sleeping mutt on the way, kicked off his sandals, and scrambled into the house. Shortly an old man came out of the house, bowing as he approached, with the little shaver clutching his trouser leg. The old guy opened the warehouse and we searched it. This being the last of them, we returned to the truck.

We proceeded on, our next job being to search the Mitsubishi Copper and Zinc Mine, which was quite a way back in the mountains. All along the way, the people we met would bow to us like frat pledges and the little kids would run and hide. If we spoke to any of the people, most of them seemed half afraid to talk. The Jap propagandists, during the war, must have really told these people some cannibalistic whoppers about the Marine Corps. Cheese n' crackers! There's nothing very carnivorous or savage looking about a fuzzy-cheeked chick like me. It's a wonder they didn't laugh.

About noon, after crossing a bridge over the Ono Gawa (a tributary of the river flowing through Takeda), we reached the mine. It was situated in a narrow, deep-cut gorge, on three sides of which were lofty mountains. The summits of most of them were blanketed by clouds. The ore refineries and the mining town were nestled against one side of the gorge.

We stopped the truck in front of the mine's head office. We took our C rations and walked into the office. Boy, did we create a turmoil! Those people couldn't have been more surprised if Boris Karloff had come gliding in on roller skates juggling atomic bombs. A secretary at a desk near the door looked up and she was so startled that her specs slid right off her nose. Another clerk standing on a stepladder, placing books on a shelf, nearly fell off. Almost instantly there were people all around us bobbing up and down in that usual "Allah, Allah" style. Honest, I felt like the emperor.

Sam, our S-2 man, explained to the mine manager, who spoke pretty good English, that we had come to look over the mine and that we meant no harm. The manager was a nervous, edgy little man who seemed afraid that we were going to gnaw the joint off its foundation. We gave our C rations to a Nip to heat up and sat down around a charcoal crock. Sam began questioning the manager about the mine, taking notes for a written report on the mine's activities, functions, etc. The Jap office force stood sheepishly around saying not a word. I drew a little cartoon of one of the secretaries. She giggled and some of the tension was broken. U.S. Army mining engineers had made a tour of the mine about two months ago and we were the first since then.

While we were eating, a timid woman appeared with a baby in her arms. With the aid of the manager, she explained that the baby was very sick and she pleaded with us to take her and the baby to the hospital at Takeda. Well, it was easy to see that the baby was sick, as she was coughing and gagging and spitting blood. Corporal Jack Jones, in charge of our group, said O.K., so the woman and her baby, Yagi our driver, and one fellow from our group hopped into the truck and headed back for town. Well, this pleased the people no end and that night they threw us a big suki yaki supper. By the time the truck made the trip to Takeda and back, it was dark, so we made arrangements to spend the night at the mine, as night time was no time to be running around those mountain roads.

We were entertained at the house of the mayor of the mining town. We removed our shoes and sat cross-legged on a mat-covered floor and were served suki yaki in little bowls. We ate with (or should I say "wrestled with") chop sticks. Suki yaki is made from chopped beef, radishes, greens resembling spinach called "horenso", and sugar. It's plenty good when made right, and the mayor's wife really knew how to prepare the stuff. Saki was also served. Saki is a wine made from rice (and it feels like it's going down sideways). Some of the town's prominent citizens were there. Two little Jap girls did some dances and everybody had a pretty good time.

The mayor got so crocked on saki that he couldn't find his house, so Jones and Houston went along with him to help him out as the old boy was really on the magic carpet. A few other Nips who attended the party went along too and most of them were in an inebriated state comparable to their mayor's. As they were crossing a high bridge, one of the Nips, a former army officer, suddenly turned on Jack Jones and tried to push him off the bridge. However Jack (an ex-lumberjack from Seattle, Washington) had other ideas about the situation and he flipped the Jap over his shoulder and off the bridge. The mayor protested, so Sam Houston flipped the mayor off. A couple of the other Nips, in their drunken state, seemed all disposed to join in, but when they saw the mayor and the other Jap land with an indignant splash in the stream below, they were somewhat discouraged to say the least.

I had been out looking for one of the fellows in our group who had a little "mata taksan" (too much) *(Nat later named one of our pet cats "Taksan" because she was too much)* and had wandered off somewhere. In the course of my search, I came upon the bridge in time to see the mayor and the former Nip army officer start on their solo flights to the stream under the bridge. The other Nips on the bridge muttered alcoholically and weaved homeward. The mayor and his buddy crawled out of the stream and staggered into the nearest house. The mayor, we were told, is a confirmed soak and sleeps in a different house every night. His wife only sees him about one night a week and that's only when he stumbles into his own house by accident.

We found our wandering buddy and Jack, Sam et al went back to the mayor's house. Yagi, our driver, came in with an arm-load of bedding and we hit the sack.

The next morning the mayor showed up, bandaged in several places; he was very apologetic about the night before. He also apologized for his tomodachi (buddy), the former officer, who was now indisposed, horizontally!!! (hangover, or should I say "throw over"). Jones just laughed and said, "O.K., Pop." I think Jack enjoyed it. We've learned one thing about the Japs here. Even though they're sly and given to treachery, they know better than to willingly molest us, because if they did, they'd have to settle for it pretty doggone stiffly. There are two main cases in which they may get violent: when they're drunk and when they're desperate for food, clothes, etc. The main time to be really on your toes is when they're drunk. There is a lot of resentment among the Japanese, but they know enough to control it because we haven't made it near as tough on them as we could make it.

Well, anyhow, we searched out the ore refineries, processors and other buildings and examined their explosives. Then I rode way back into the mine tunnel in a little electric car to a 700-foot shaft where work was being done by compressed air drills. Most of the work is done by small boys. Then I returned to the truck where the rest were waiting, climbed aboard, and we shoved off yelling "sayonara" (goodbye).

We got back to the hotel in Takeda in time for evening chow, after which I took a bath at a Jap bath house reserved for our use and then hit the sack and read a while.

On the next two days we patrolled two small towns near Takeda. First we went out to Kiyi and searched out some warehouses, barns and a school. Next we went to Miyada, mounted horses and rode around the base of a large mountain. After searching a few mills and barns, we returned to Miyada and stopped at a small hotel, the only one in town. Yagi then said, "Me fix, hokay". He then disappeared inside and went "yappity, yappity, yappity" to the proprietor, and soon we were inside squatting around a long, short-legged table and the old Nip hotel proprietor was hopping here and there serving suki yaki, and Yagi was playing a harmonica and skipping a sprightly Japanese dance step. Yagi was quite the boy.

No patrols went out for the next two days, as the Japs were holding national elections of Diet members. They ran the elections themselves. All we did was to stand by in case of riots and also to look out for anybody attempting to buy votes. It was the first time that Jap women have been permitted to vote and they were pretty excited about it.

As I said before, we hit Takeda at the time of the cherry blossom festival and we went to several suki yaki and saki parties around town. Boy, do those Nips go off their trolley when they throw a party! The men threw each other through the doors and the women did wild dances while caressing saki bottles. The cherry blossom festival is the only time that the women are allowed to drink with the men at parties.

I didn't drink much saki, but quite a few of the fellows in our patrol stowed away a pretty sizeable tank-load of the stuff and, after the parties broke up, they usually would feel pretty playful. On our next to last night there, a group of fellows with a considerable snoot full went for a bike ride. Waving their saki bottles, they crashed through the front doors of a small hotel down the street from ours. They all wound up in a heap at the foot of the staircase. Total casualties: four bumped heads, two broken ribs, two smashed doors, one indignant hotel manager and three smashed bottles of saki (which was the most deeply mourned mishap). They were seven "beat" guys when they finally got back. Another bunch of Gyrene gents in their cups played a rather haphazard softball game on the hotel's rooftop observation porch. Nearly all were clad in naught but their drawers, all except for one hardy soul who was clad in naught (period). There were some "oki atamas" (big heads) the next morning.

On our last day, being we had covered all our area, we just drove out into the mountains and had some target practice with our rifles. On our way back to town a slight accident occurred. The roads were a bit slippery from the night before when it rained from about midnight till about seven in the morning. As we rounded a sharp turn, the truck skidded and sideswiped into the cliff. Now don't worry! The only damages inflicted were a few new dents in the truck and a broken cigarette holder that a Jap gave to Alex.

We returned to the hotel, ate noon chow, and went down to the railroad station. Our lieutenant hopped on board the train and, turning to us, said, "OK, dead end kids! Climb aboard!". Gawsh! Whatta life.

There goes taps. I've been writing this all day in my spare moments.
Love to you all, Bunk

****

Oita, Japan
April 20, 1946

Dear Mother,

Last night we got some official word passed on to us. The 2nd Marine Division is leaving Japan. The moving-out date has been set at June 1st. The 2nd Marines, being the senior regiment of the division, will go first as the forward echelon. The 6th, 8th and 10th Marines (the other regiments composing the division) will follow later along with other attached battalions. The Army is due to relieve us here around the first of June.

That's all the official scoop we were given. We weren't even told where we're going., but everyone is pretty certain that the division is going home, as the 2nd Marines Division was formed overseas way back before the Guadalcanal campaign and has never done duty in the States as a unit. However, whether I will return home with the division is doubtful. There have been strong rumors that low-point reserves and regulars will be dropped off at Guam in the Marianas to form an outpost brigade. Then again, Milt Gillespie, my Buddy from Georgia, is a clerk in the battalion adjutant's office and he picked up some fairly reliable scuttlebutt through headquarters to the effect that all hands, low-pointers, etc. of the division will return home if the division goes back.

There it is. We're definitely leaving Japan around June 1st after being relieved by Army Occupation Troops. The rest is rumor, but we're hoping for the best. Please don't be over hopeful but keep your fingers crossed. Things look pretty encouraging.

I'm glad to hear that my box arrived home at last *(Nat mailed this box in mid-February from Miyakonojo, so his prediction of two months in transit was accurate.)* I was surprised to learn that everything was in pretty good shape, as I've seen those post office lads in action - rough boys!

I was also glad that Pop's shoulder is getting better. I know how he hates to be tied down with any ailment.

The mail must still be a bit snafu. Two letters that I mailed to Aunt Fanny Cockey *(he had to specify ... he had three Aunts Fanny!)* and one that I wrote to Aunt Sis were returned to me. They were sent to someplace in Missouri. Next time I'll print "Maryland" in full instead of abbreviating it. Did *(Cousin)* Bill ever receive that letter I sent him from Pearl Harbor with the programs of all the football and baseball games I saw there? The F.P.O. probably sent that to Madagascar.

I'm in charge of a Nip working party today so I've gotta go.
Love to you all, Bunk

****

Oita, Japan
April 27, 1946

Dear "Runt",

Here it is birthday number six already. Imagine that! Gosh, you're getting to be too big a girl to call "Runt". Why, the way you're sprouting up, when I get home you'll probably be able to look down at me and say, "For the luvva Mike, Shorty! When are you gonna grow?!"

I wish I could reach out right now and pull those long pigtails and hear you giggle in that way that makes a guy tickle all over.

Bonnie, I'm a little too far away to celebrate this one with you but don't you worry, we'll make up for it. When I get back we'll really step out. If Glen Echo is still open *(it was - and still is in 2010!)*, we'll ride the merry-go-round and racer dips till they wear out. Or maybe we will buy a big bag of peanuts and go to a downtown movie. Then we'll sit down at the soda fountain at People's and order the biggest plate of ice cream you ever saw. If you'd like it, we'll ride the bus out to the Zoo. We'll really have a time, won't we?

Give your old man a hot foot, box a few rounds with your sister, plant a loud, smacking kiss on your Mother and Granny, blow all those birthday candles out on that cake and have a happy birthday all day long.

Love, Bunk

* * * *

Oita, Japan
(Sun.) April 28, 1946

Dear Pat,

Things are snappin' and poppin' around here. The quartermaster, armory, company property shed and all, are busy packing gear, taking inventory and measuring for shipping space. It's pretty definite that the 2nd Division is going back to the States. However, the possibility of my returning home with the division hangs doubtfully in the balance. During the past few days, reports, rumors, etc. have been going around (as they have an obnoxious habit of doing) pretty strong to the effect that low-point reserves and regulars will be left behind, probably at Guam (ugh!), to form an outpost brigade. Even a couple of our platoon sergeants who don't usually commit themselves one way or the other about scuttlebutt, have said that they think that is probably what will happen. However, they don't really know.

Yet, contrary to the scuttlebutt I've just related to you, Milt Gillespie and several other clerks in the battalion office still contend that all reserves, points or no points, will go back with the division, basing their dope on information picked up through headquarters. So there you have it. Nobody seems to know anything definite, and the higher-ups won't tell us anything other than that the division is pulling out. The wild tales concerning who's going where are, like the proverbial clinkers, really stacking up. Everyone is so tired of rumors that this morning Woj asked me what time it was and when I told him 9:15, he said, "Aw, bull**CENSORED**, I don't believe it! It's probably scuttlebutt!"

Right now I don't know where I stand. However, I should know something definite soon.

I'm almost sorry that I wrote such an optimistic letter to Mother last time, as she may become over hopeful. However, there's one fairly certain thing. If by chance I should be left behind somewhere when the division goes home, I'm reasonably sure that I would eventually get home by September. Anyhoo, Miss Bertie, keep your fingers crossed and maybe I'll come klip-klopping home on sandals with my buck teeth sticking out pretty soon.

Zig and Alex are yelping for me to go to the PX with them We just have time to make it before going on guard. It's raining clinkers outside and if we catch the ebb tide it shouldn't take over 4 days to skip the rapids to the PX.

I gotta trot off now before they get impatient and pull off one of my stray limbs and bludgeon me with it.
Sayonara
Love, Nat

P.S. Enclosed is a 2nd Division patch. This one is of the original design, slightly different from the other one I sent you which is the newer design. Thought you might like one of each kind.

****

Oita, Japan
(Sun.) May 5, 1946

Dear Mother,

Spring is really here now and the countryside is green all over. It rains pretty often but the days are getting warmer and balmier all the time. The country is prettier now than I've seen it so far. The trees are billowy and fully dressed in leaves, and the rice and grain in the paddies is nearly hip high and bright green. The Japanese, as you know, are flower fanciers and usually even the humblest of homes has a few flowers of some sort blooming around it. There's a type pf rose tree that blooms plentifully around here. Sure is pretty.

This afternoon, a large group of Jap kids from the Beppu Convent performed on the stage of our camp theater. Their ages ranged from 6 to 12. They sang songs and did folk dances. They sure were cute and received a big hand from the fellows. The kids are the most likeable of Japs because when they're small, they're just natural, unsophisticated, amiable kids who are too young to entertain any convictions or orneriness like older Nips.

An Army regiment is due to arrive here in a couple of days which means our regiment will move out to Sasebo, Kyushu's main port, soon. When we get there, we'll find out definitely who is going back to the States with the division when it sails in June. As it stands now, I have about a 50-50 chance of going. However, as I said before, nobody seems to know definitely and the scuttlebutt is flying thick and fast. I hope my other letters about this "division going home" business haven't caused any over-speculation among you-all. Nevertheless, we can hope for the best. At any rate, as I said in my last letter, if I am left behind somewhere over here when the division sails, I should be home at least by September.

These playful apes in my squad room are staging a miniature sham battle and hurling everything from steel helmets to chow gear around. I just missed having my hair parted by a canteen so I better quit and go take a shower while I still have my limbs intact

So-o-o-o-o
Oyasumi (goodnight)
& Love to you all, Bunk

****

Oita, Japan

(Sun.) May 12, 1946

Dear Mother,

Today, just as a lot of fellows on Mother's Day are doing, I'm thinking of you. I'm thinking about those duck dinners and lemon pies, and the trouble you had getting me out of the sack and pushing me out the front door to make the 8:45 bus, and the way you'd hustle cheerfully here and there with Pepsi Cola and sandwiches whenever the frat was at the house and you'd be laughing, even though we were wrecking the joint.

Gosh, I guess I caused you 99% of your gray hairs. And don't you worry about those gray hairs! You wear them beautifully and they definitely do <u>not</u> make you look old. You're the prettiest Mammy of 'em all. "Wakarimaska?" (You understand?).

Doggone, I wish I could have sent you something, but during the latter part of April, an order stating that no more packages could be sent home was issued. But when I get back, I'll bring you sump'm real purty, you betcha'!

Units of the 24th Army division are starting to arrive here from Shikoku, the smallest of the 4 main Jap home islands. Our outfit entrains for Sasebo on May 26th. We won't be there very long and I should know soon after getting there how I stand in regard to going home with the 2nd Division.

Alex and Milt are waiting for me to go to church with them s-o-o have a happy Momma's day and "Watakshi wa anata wo ai shite imas" (I love you).

Sayonara, Bunk

✷✷✷✷

(This letter to sister Pat w/ one especially poetic paragraph, is dated May 20,1946, 6 years to the day before Nat & I met & I fell in love at first sight. Nat said later he did, too, but it took him a while to realize it! Although this outing really occurred, the telling has more than a bit of the "Tall Tale" to it.)

Oita, Japan
(Mon.) May 20, 1946

Dear Pat,

Today finds me walking like a pair of pliers as I spent yesterday afternoon horseback riding in the hills in back of Beppu. I think my horse was a fugitive from a Bing Crosby movie. Not that he was slow, but on our way up through the grain paddies, two snails, three caterpillars and a toad passed us. My patience was finally exhausted when a centipede with 99 of its legs in plaster casts left us in the dust. So I said, "Look here, Old Ironsides, you better shift into high and make more knots than this or else our mess sergeant will catch up with you and it would undoubtedly hurt your equestrian pride to find yourself in the same pot with a lot of Spam." To which the horse sharply retorted, "Oh yeah! He can't hurt me. I'm a union horse, and we've got John L. Lewis' old man in our stables to prove it. He's in the stall next to mine!" *(Nat did not know then, that for nearly 60 years he would be an important union activist.)* Well, enough of this horse play (hay! hay!) and more about the scenery.

Honest, it was really something to see. Yesterday was warm and balmy, one of those days that makes you just want to wander around aimlessly. The mountains a short distance away had a green, spongy molded look and their grassy slopes looked smooth as a pool table. There was a lazy blue haze over the coastal valley slope and everything had a sleepy appearance. The houses nestled in the hillsides or among the paddies looked as if they were dozing in the sun. After riding further up into the hills I could overlook the terraced grain paddies and, gawsh, it was just like looking down a green, corduroy stair case.

There are countless hot springs around Beppu. I passed several while wandering around. I rode up to an alligator farm near one of the hot springs. The 'gators were dozing in the specially built ponds. There sure were a lot of potential suitcases there. Some were pretty big, a couple of them about 12 feet long. I prodded one with a stout pole and he snapped it in two like a pretzel. Sweet disposition, what?

I came across some pretty homes in the country around Beppu. They were built mostly of stout cedar and sometimes white plaster and had expensive tile roofs. Nearly all had small, well-kept patios or courtyards. These suburban homes are owned mostly by rich landlords. However, at one time, a lot of big industrialists and businessmen from up on Honshu, the main island, owned pretty homes down here at Beppu. They used to come here for treatments at the hot springs. During normal times, Beppu was one of the most popular summer resorts in Japan, which accounts for the presence of a lot of hotels.

Ol' Ironsides, the nag I was riding, proved to be an amiable animal. He was slow and easy-going and wouldn't hurry "fer nawthin", which proved to be satisfactory as all I had to do was sit back and watch. It was one of the best days I've spent in Japan.

I guess things are pretty well snappin' and poppin' around school, with proms, graduation, competitive drill, etc. comin' up. The preparations are slight headaches but the results are a lot of fun.

Chow time. Gotta run.

Love, Nat

****

Oita, Japan
(Sun.) May 26, 1946

Dear Mother,

My sea bag is packed, my bedding is rolled up and tied, and my pack is made up. Tonight at six we board the train for a 12-hour ride to Sasebo. Everyone is sitting around waiting for chow call, after which we load on the trucks and shove off for the train station. All our cots are folded and have been placed outside, so we are sitting on our packs. Some of the fellows are playing cards. Whitey and Woj are throwing a softball around, and Alex and Zig are playfully wrenching each other's limbs. Sprightly bunch of gremlins, what?

The train ride to Sasebo won't be particularly comfortable, as the cars are dirty and the seats are straight-backed like streetcar seats. However, even though we probably won't get much sleep, we can pass the time by singing and clowning around and stuff like that there. Also, a couple guys in my platoon got some new movie magazines in the mail and they always prove interesting

(hubba! hubba!).

The Army has taken over the camp and the joint is full of doggies (soldiers).

A couple of minutes till chow, so I better quit for now. Next stop, Sasebo!

Love, Bunk

****

Sasebo, Japan
(*Wed.*) May 29, 1946

Dear Mother,

    The 2ⁿᵈ Regt. is settled in Sasebo, Kyushu's main seaport. We are quartered in Quonset huts built by the Sea Bees. The Sea Bees have this place fixed up pretty well. Besides good quarters, there's a good movie hall, a couple of basketball courts, and a swimming pool nearby. There is a battalion of Sea Bees living in this camp, but Marines and Sea Bees get along O.K., as everywhere the Corps fought there were nearly always some Sea Bees there, too.

    I've found out where Woodie is quartered. He's in 2ⁿᵈ Signal Co. here in Sasebo. I'm going to go see him as soon as I get liberty. Since arriving here Mon. morning, I've seen quite a few fellows that came overseas with me and who are stationed in Division Headquarters Battalion, M.P.s, Engineers, etc. here at Sasebo.

    Right now we're not doing anything much, but in a day or two we'll get some ship-loading jobs. We have already resumed guard duty, but the camp guard here is smaller and requires fewer posts and less men, so I won't have to stand post as often as at Oita, where the guard was larger.

    Well, I've got to go on guard in about an hour so I better go take a shower while I have time.

    More later and

Love to you all, Bunk

✳✳✳✳

Sasebo, Japan
(Sun.) June 2, 1946

Dear Mother,

I went on liberty the other day and I saw Woodie. He is a telephone operator in the division headquarters building and it sure is funny to hear him say, "Num-bah, plee-uz", Alabama style. We had a lot to talk about. He was an electrician before he entered the corps and this helped him a great deal in his work with the Signal Co. Woodie is a regular and expects probably to be sent to China soon.

"Alex", "Whitey" and "Woj" are also regulars and they, along with the other short-time regulars of this outfit, left yesterday to join a special draft of regulars which will leave Japan, possibly for China, soon. That busts up the partnership of White, Wynstra, Wojculewicz, Wright and Zieglmeier, Inc. "Whitey", "Alex", "Woj", "Zig" and I have been together from the time we left San Diego, California till now and it was a sad day when they split us up. We called ourselves the "Fee-ro-cious Five". When Woodie was with us, we were known as the "Sad Sack Sextet", but after he was transferred out of our outfit at Nagasaki, we had to take a new title. "Zig" is a reserve and he and I will remain together.

And now comes some important data. Our lieutenant told us that the 2nd Marines, our regiment, are scheduled to land on the east coast of the U.S., possibly at Norfolk, after a 35-day voyage which takes in the Panama Canal. I'm almost afraid to say anything for fear that something might happen at the last minute but, as far as I know, I will go along with the outfit when it sails for the States.

I recently found out that I am eligible for discharge September 1st, which is a contributing reason for my returning home with the outfit. So keep your fingers crossed and hope that there's no last-minute change. This outfit is pretty unpredictable.

We start loading ships soon. We haven't been told the sailing date, but the consensus of opinion is that it will be between the 6th and the 10th. At any rate, it should be soon.

It's starting to rain so I better go get my clothes off the line. I showed some downright domestic qualities today when I did a pretty big wash. I am hereby open to any attractive matrimonial bids. Step right up, gals! hurry! hurry!

So long & Love to you all, Bunk

****

(This was Nat's last letter from Japan. He had been on the Japanese island of Kyushu for 6½ months)

Sasebo, Japan
(Wed.) June 12, 1946

Dear Mother,

Today's the big day. At one o'clock I board the ship, homeward bound! It doesn't seem possible, but it is. I haven't much time as I've got some last-minute packing to do. Here's some pertinent scoop about the trip.

The trip will take about 35 days. We are going down through the Panama Canal and up to Norfolk, Va. From Norfolk we will go down to Camp Lejeune, N.C. (Ugh! Looks like I can't escape that place!). I don't know whether I'll get a furlough or leave right away or not. But, at any rate, I won't be at Camp Lejeune very long, as I am eligible for discharge after Sept. 2nd. Also, there're always those week-end liberties, so I'll get home one way or another as soon as possible after our regiment gets situated in the States.

I've gotta get back to my packing so I better quit for now.

So long and "See ya soon",
Love to you all, Bunk

****

U.S.S. Lavaca (at sea)
(Fri.) June 21, 1946

Dear Mother,

We've almost completed the first leg of our homeward trip. On June 23rd, Sunday, we dock at Pearl Harbor for 24 hours to take on supplies, fuel, etc. and then we go on to Panama. We have covered over 4000 miles so far on our voyage and have been at sea about 10 days. From Pearl Harbor to Panama is about 4700 miles and will take about 12 days. (You'll have to excuse this lop-sided penmanship as we have run into some fairly rough sea. This page has been sprayed a couple of times already). The whole regiment, about 1700 men, has been crammed aboard this ship, a combat transport which isn't nearly as large as the ship I went from San Diego to Pearl Harbor on. However, we're all pretty well used to crowded shipboard routine and anyway we're headed home, so we ain't complainin'.

The trip through the Panama Canal should prove to be very interesting and I know I'll get a bang out of it. I'll write from there.

When we get to the states my address will be:

Co. F, 2nd Bn., 2nd Marines
2nd Marine Division
Camp Lejeune N.C.

I've got to give this to our company mail clerk so he can mail it at Pearl Harbor.

So long for now,
Love to you all, Bunk

* * * *

(This was the last saved letter of Nat's short military hitch. There were no additional letters saved from [or about] the voyage. Nat was discharged a few days earlier than anticipated, 8/23/46)